THE WAR AND THE BAGDAD RAILWAY

THE STORY OF ASIA MINOR AND ITS RELATION TO THE PRESENT CONFLICT

BY

MORRIS JASTROW, Jr., Ph.D., LL.D.

PROFESSOR IN THE UNIVERSITY OF PENNSYLVANIA
AUTHOR OF "THE CIVILIZATION OF BABYLONIA AND ASSYRIA," ETC.

WITH 14 ILLUSTRATIONS
AND A MAP

"Hard Days, Sword Days, Death Days."
(VAULUNDURS SAGA)

THIRD IMPRESSION

PHILADELPHIA

J. B. LIPPINCO

D1161708

COPYRIGHT, 1917, BY J. B. LIPPINCOTT COMPANY
COPYRIGHT, 1918, BY J. B. LIPPINCOTT COMPANY

PUBLISHED NOVEMBER, 1917
SECOND IMPRESSION, FEBRUARY, 1918
THIRD IMPRESSION, APRIL, 1918

PRINTED BY J. B. LIPPINCOTT COMPANY
AT THE WASHINGTON SQUARE PRESS
PHILADELPHIA, U. S. A.

THE WAR AND THE BAGDAD RAILWAY

THE STORY OF ASIA MINOR AND ITS RELATION TO THE PRESENT CONFLICT

BY THE SAME AUTHOR

THE CIVILIZATION OF BABYLONIA AND ASSYRIA

ITS REMAINS, LANGUAGE, HISTORY, RELIGION, COMMERCE, LAW, ART AND LITERATURE

BY

MORRIS JASTROW, Jr., Ph.D., LL.D.

Professor of Semitic Languages, University of Pennsylvania

With map and 164 illustrations. Octavo. Gilt top, in a box. Net $7.00.

ART AND ARCHÆOLOGY:—"This magnificent book gives a comprehensive and complete survey of the whole civilization of the ancient peoples, who dwelt in the Tigro-Euphrates Valley. It is written by one of the foremost Semitic scholars of the world, and supersedes all works upon the subject. Written in the author's characteristic lucid style, it is sumptuously illustrated, and is a beautiful specimen of bookmaking.

TO THE
MEMBERS OF THE WEDNESDAY
MORNING CLUB OF PITTSFIELD, MASS.
WITH MANY PLEASANT MEMORIES

19060

PREFACE TO THE SECOND IMPRESSION

I AVAIL myself of the publication of a second printing of this work (without any changes in the text) to amplify somewhat the distinction between the war as it appeared in 1914 and its aspect in 1917, which I set forth at the beginning of the concluding chapter. The distinction made between what I call the two wars is, as I can see, open to an interpretation which was remote from my mind. The main purpose of this concluding chapter is to bring forward a proposed solution for the Eastern Question, suggested as the result of a prolonged study both of the ancient and of the modern East. By way of leading up to this solution I felt it desirable to emphasize that the various issues which confronted Europe at the outbreak of the war in 1914,—and among which, as I endeavored to show, the Bagdad Railway was the largest single contributing factor,—have been moved into the background through the supreme and paramount issue which became more sharply defined as the war progressed. This paramount issue, the existence of a ruthless militarism in close alliance with an entirely antiquated form of autocratic government, is essentially a moral one, for the attempt to terrorize the world and to carry out a national policy of domination through sheer military force are two cardinal sins against what may be called the conscience of the world.

It is not the first time that such a menace has confronted the world, but it may safely be asserted that the menace has never appeared in so formidable a guise. The world cannot pursue its even course until the spectre of Prussian militarism has been laid. The paramount issue, as I indicate in my volume, must be disposed of first, before the questions confronting Europe during the fateful last week of July can be taken up.

In drawing a distinction, therefore, between the two wars, I did not wish to imply that there was no connection between them. On the contrary I indicated that the main factor leading to the recognition on the part of the civilized world of the paramount issue was Germany's brutal and inexcusable conduct of the war which revealed her sinister plans, formed long before 1914, for forceful domination of the East without regard to the simplest demands of international law or to the most elementary considerations of humanitarianism. The purpose of these plans was by means of such domination to establish for herself the commanding place in the world to the discomfiture and virtual subjugation of her rivals.

Writing as a student of history, whose primary obligation is to present the various sides of a situation clearly and fairly before pronouncing a verdict, I give, in the course of the discussion, Germany's side of the diplomatic position as it appeared on August 1st, 1914, that is to say, at the time of the declaration of war on Russia; and I do this in order to emphasize that giving Germany the full benefit of every doubt,— on the assumption that she was entirely sincere in the presentation of her case in the White Book issued by the German Government shortly after the outbreak of the war,—she would still be condemned in the eyes of the world by her *conduct* of the war, which spoilt any case that she might have had.

My indictment represents the *verdict* after a review of her case. We might, as I suggest in the same connection, go even so far as to waive the question whether she actually *willed* the war, and assume that the pressure of the military party on the civil government forced the issue (and for which there is some evidence), and yet we would have to condemn her just as strongly because of her unwillingness to *prevent* the war by her fateful and criminal rejection of Sir Edward Grey's proposition for a conference to settle the Austrian-Servian crisis and to which conference all the other powers had consented.

Concerned as I am in this closing chapter, as throughout the book, with the Eastern Question, I did not deem it necessary to enlarge on the more general aspects of the war (particularly as my views on that phase have merely the value of the ordinary observer), or I would have emphasized strongly, instead of merely suggesting as I do, that Germany's support of Austria's contention that the Servian question was a matter for her to settle without European intervention, had a sinister substratum. That sinister substratum is, of course, more clearly evident now, in 1917, than it was in 1914, though at that time it was no doubt recognized in the European Chancelleries, familiar with the details of Germany's plan for domination of the East. The railway from Berlin-Vienna-Constantinople leads through Belgrade, Nish and Sofia. The control of Servia, as of Bulgaria, was, therefore, essential to Germany for carrying out the Hamburg to Bagdad project, the very core of Pan-Germanism, as I point out towards the close of the chapter on the Bagdad Railway.

At the same time, while it is evident that the Bagdad Railway project was thus the deciding factor that led Germany in July, 1914, to take the position that directly brought on the war as an inevitable outcome of that position, it must be recognized by the historian —as it is indeed recognized by all thoughtful students—that there were other issues, of a most serious and threatening character, that helped to complicate the situation in Europe and that contained the menace of an Inter-European war. No one can read Mr. Lowes Dickinson's careful analysis of the European situation in 1914, as succinctly set forth in his " European Anarchy," to which I refer several times in the course of my book, or read the account of the diplomatic negotiations in M. P. Price's Diplomatic History of the War, or any other of a dozen books that might be mentioned, without realizing the combustible material that lay loosely about in the diplomatic workshops of Europe in 1914. It is only necessary to name the Balkan question, which had brought on two serious conflicts in two successive years shortly before 1914, and to refer to the admirable investigation of the complicated problem that has recently been published by Mr. J. A. R. Marriott (" The Eastern Question, A Study in European Diplomacy," Oxford, 1917) to warn us against a onesided view by concentrating our *exclusive* attention on Germany's aggressive plans. The ambitions of Russia—at the time under the sway of an imperialistic group of much the same type as in Germany—to secure Constantinople and to form a Pan-Slavonic union to thwart Germany's ambitions and to check the plans of Austria-Hungary for the Balkan control, cannot, of course, be overlooked in a survey of the European situation in 1914. Italy, too, had been growing restless for a slice of the East. In 1911 she had seized Tripoli, which had brought on her war with Turkey. She was laying plans for a zone of influence along the southern coast of Asia Minor and she manifested a direct and aggressive interest in the Albanian question. The growing economic rivalry between England and Germany for the markets of the world was another issue that, to be sure, was not disassociated from the political ambitions of Germany, for the German government was behind the commercial expansion plans of her manufacturers and merchants, ready to aid them in order to strengthen her political hold over her own population, but the rivalry nevertheless was an outcome of conditions that did not have their origin in diplomatic complications. It seems to me, therefore, that to distinguish sharply between the aspect of the war in 1914 and the aspect which it has in 1917 is helpful to a clarification of the situation—That is what I had in mind in representing the contrast as that between two wars. The paramount issue in the present aspect of the war, so clearly defined in the various notable utterances of the official spokesman of this republic during 1917 and 1918, was, of course, present also in the war of 1914, but as an *undercurrent* which was brought to the surface through the three factors on which I dwell at the beginning of the closing chapter, to wit: Germany's conduct of the war, the Russian Revolution, and our entrance into the conflict.

The rivalry for supremacy among the great European nations is assuredly a fact that cannot be denied, as little as the fact that all of them—Russia, England, France, Italy and even Greece—had their national ambitions in 1914 and long before that period, as well as Germany and Austria-Hungary. These ambitions took on different forms, a longing for more territory in some cases, a desire for political control of a region in others, and an ambition for spheres of commercial influence with or without political control in still others. Conflicting ambitions are as natural among nations as are rivalries in the non-political commercial world. When these conflicting ambitions reach a crisis, war is always imminent, and under the historical conditions that held sway in Europe prior to 1914, it may be said that war is almost inevitable. Witness the fact that the nineteenth century, despite its glorious achievements in science and its marvelous material progress through discoveries and inventions that have revolutionized the aspect of life, has more wars to its credit—or rather, to its discredit—than almost any other century in the world's history.

It is not easy, without an effort, to project ourselves back to 1914 without being influenced by the viewpoint that has developed in 1917. It is quite natural that we should look at 1914 from the vantage ground of the development of the war, but if we make the effort to visualize conditions three and a half years ago as they then appeared to the surface observer, there is, I feel, considerable justification for regarding the war of 1914—viewed from the point of view of 1914, and not of 1917—as a struggle for supremacy among European nations, brought about, in the last analysis, as the result of conflicting national ambitions, with Germany's aggressive policy for domination in the East, under the threat and menace of the mailed fist, as the chief factor, but not as the only one, in leading to the conflict that has plunged the world in such sorrow and suffering.

We may, at the present moment, look hopefully towards the future. The message, voiced so effectively by President Wilson, presaging the dawn of a new era in which the rights of nations to life and liberty will receive the first consideration, and in which the will of the people will be the sovereign force everywhere, is sweeping like a mighty current through the world. That message is penetrating even the thick walls that the Central Powers have erected around themselves to prevent their people from hearing the new gospel. It may be that these walls will have to be stormed at the point of the bayonet and amidst the roar of cannon before the message can reach Germany and Austria-Hungary in all its force, but of the ultimate triumph of the higher principle in the regulation of international relations, announced over two thousand years ago by a Hebrew prophet, " Not by might nor by power, but by my spirit "—of the triumph of the *idea,* through its inherent force, and stripped of all shining armor—there need be no doubt and there need be no fear.

M. J., Jr.

Philadelphia, February, 1918

PREFACE TO THE FIRST IMPRESSION

THE purpose of this volume is to elucidate an aspect of the war which although it is overshadowed at present by the paramount issue—the menace of a militarism in league with autocracy—was the most significant single factor contributing to the outbreak of the long-foreseen war in 1914, and will form one of the most momentous problems when the time for the peace negotiations arrives. Ever since the announcement was made towards the close of the year 1899 that the Turkish government had conceded to a German syndicate the privilege of building a railway to connect Constantinople with Bagdad through a transverse route across Asia Minor, the Bagdad Railway has been the core of the Eastern Question. There were to be sure other aspects of that question, which led to the two Balkan wars of 1912 and 1913, but the addition of the Bagdad Railway was an aggravating factor to an already sufficiently complicated situation that involved the great European powers—England, France, Germany and Russia—in a network of diplomatic negotiations, the meshes of which became closer as the years rolled on. The railway became the spectre of the twentieth century. It was a spectre that always appeared armed " from top to toe " and when occasionally he " wore his beaver up," the face was that of a grim, determined warrior.

As an industrial enterprise, the project of a railway through a most notable historic region, and passing along a route which had resounded to the tread of armies thousands of years ago, was fraught with great possibilities of usefulness in opening up the nearer East to brisk trade with Europe that would follow in the wake of the locomotive, and in infusing the young Western spirit into the old East, carrying western ideas, western modes of education, and western science to the mother-lands of civilization. The railway would also prove to be a short cut to India and the farther East, and as such the undertaking was on a plane of importance with the cutting of the Suez Canal. Connecting through junctions and branches with the other railway systems of Asia Minor, Syria and Palestine, the Bagdad Railway would result in covering the entire region with a perfect network of modern methods of transportation that would embrace eventually also the projected railways of Persia. Full credit should be given to the German brains in which this project was hatched, and there is no reason to suspect that at the outset, the German *capitalists* who fathered the enterprise were actuated by any other motive than the perfectly legitimate one to create a great avenue of commerce. When, however, the German government entered the field as the backer and promoter of the scheme, the political aspect of the railway was moved into the foreground, and that aspect has since overshadowed the commercial one. The full political import of the Bagdad Railway becomes apparent in the light of the eventful history of Asia Minor which can now be followed, at least in general outlines, from a period as early as 2000 B.C. To illustrate the main thesis suggested by the route of the railway that the control of the historic highway stretching from Constantinople to Bagdad has at all times involved the domination of the Near East, it has been necessary to sketch the history of Asia

Minor in its relation to the great civilizations of antiquity and to follow that history through the period of Greek, Roman, Parthian and Arabic control, past the efforts of the Crusaders to save the route for Christian Europe, to the final conquest of it by the Ottoman Turks. That event, marked by the capture of Constantinople in 1453, directly led to the discovery of America in 1492.

I feel that no apology is needed for thus devoting a large chapter of the volume to this history, for apart from its intrinsic interest, our understanding of the present situation in the Near East is dependent upon an appreciation of the position that Asia Minor, as the bridge leading to the East, has always held.

The war has resulted in bringing many countries closer to our horizon, but no lands more so than those to which Asia Minor, as I shall attempt to show, is the *Hinterland*—Mesopotamia, Syria, Arabia and Egypt. Until recently, the history of these lands has been looked upon by the general public as the domain of the specializing historian, philologist and archæologist. With the extension of the European war into these eastern lands, they become a part— and an essential part—of the general political situation. Their history needs to be known, if the problems arising from the relation of Asia Minor to the issues of the war are to be dealt with at the peace conference in an intelligent manner. I cherish the hope which, I trust, is not a delusion, that my sketch of the history of Asia Minor will help to illuminate the factors underlying " the trend towards the East " which began with Alexander the Great, which led modern nations to take possession of eastern lands, and of which the Bagdad Railway is the latest manifestation.

I have thought it proper to give the story of the Bagdad Railway in some detail, because through this we can best follow the growth of the spirit of hostile rivalry among European nations which culminated in the outbreak three years ago. A war like the present one cannot, to be sure, be carried back to any one issue, isolated from all others, but although many issues are behind the war, it is the Bagdad Railway that created the frame of mind among the European powers which made the war—one is inclined to put it—inevitable. A war breaks out when nations are ready for it—ready, I mean, in their disposition. The Bagdad Railway made them ready in this sense. The story of the Bagdad Railway tells us how this frame of mind was produced—and yet back of it all, we must bear in mind the deeper currents of history that produce the agitation on the surface.

The study of the relation of Asia Minor to the present conflict—on the basis of its history—would be incomplete without at least an attempt to peer into the future, a hazardous undertaking but which nevertheless has its value in at least suggesting the line along which the solution of the problem of the Bagdad Railway, and with it the Eastern Question of which it is the core is to be sought. As a preliminary to this outlook, I have tried to set forth the sharp distinction between what I would call the two wars—the war of 1914 and the war of 1917. The recognition of this distinction appears to me to be essential for an understanding of the situation that will arise at the time of the peace conference.

The former war is in the main the European struggle for supremacy, the latter is the great world war for the preservation and spread of the spirit

and the institutions of democracy. I am writing as
a student of history and not as a partisan, except
in so far as my position is, as I believe it to be, in
accord with the American point of view as voiced
by its most thoughtful and most sober representatives. I have no sympathy even in war time with
that blatant form of patriotism which warps one's
judgment and prevents a penetration into the deeper
meaning of this war. It is the existence of that
kind of patriotism in Germany which has produced
the Pan-Germanic spirit, and the strength of which
(though waning) prevents the German people from
even now recognizing the reason for the hostility
that they have aroused throughout the world. My
indictment, therefore, of Germany's *conduct* of the
war which has been the main factor, as I see it, leading from the war of 1914 to that of 1917, is set forth
" more in sorrow than in anger "—a sorrow that
must, I think, be shared by all who admired the
Germany before the war for her remarkable achievements in all fields, and that bears heaviest on the
thousands of Americans who, like myself, received
the training for their careers at German universities
and who feel keenly the intellectual ties that bind
them to that country. But Germany has none but
herself to blame for having thus transformed her
friends into her opponents. She first handicapped
those who were disposed at the outbreak of the war
to see and present her side sympathetically by the
violation of Belgian neutrality, she then condemned
them to silence by the atrocious treatment of the
Belgians and by the sinking of the Lusitania, and
she finally converted them into enemies in arms by
her ruthless submarine warfare that has done far
more harm to the German name than any injury

that the sink-at-sight procedure can inflict on the world's shipping. As I write these lines I have before me a monograph by a German scholar on Germany's position in the East after the two Balkan wars in 1912 and 1913. Incidental to the discussion the author gives some shocking details, vouched for by reliable witnesses, of the atrocities committed in the first of these wars by the Bulgarians and Serbians. He speaks of the systematic attempt to wipe out the Turks by wholesale massacres on a huge scale, and the author asks, in a tone of righteous indignation, whether the voice of humanitarianism and civilization can remain silent with such deeds going on? The Bulgarians are now the allies of the Germans, and in the present war the Turks seem to be following exactly the same policy towards the Armenians that the Bulgarians adopted to annihilate an entire people. Did the German government respond to the desperate cry of humanity to stop *officially* ordered massacres in Armenia? And yet the Turk is neither cruel nor—unless stirred up—fanatical. Those who have lived longest in Turkish countries and who know the Turk best bear evidence to the fine traits of his character and that under normal conditions, Turkish Moslems and Christian Armenians live quite amicably side by side. The Armenian massacres represent a part of the *policy* of the Turkish government, as the Russian *pogroms* under the old régime were always organized by the Russian government. The population is stirred up by spreading false reports of a proposed revolt on the part of the Armenians—and the rest follows. The war of 1914 as conducted by Germany forms a close parallel. The cruelties practised and the inhuman methods of warfare resorted to are part of

the military *policy,* and for which the German government, following a deliberate plan of spreading
terrorism and enforcing subordination, must bear
the responsibility. The author whom I have quoted,
assuming (as I do) that he is sincere in his denunciation of cruelties officially carried out by the Bulgarian government, ought certainly to be able to
answer the question why the whole civilized world
has changed its former admiration for Germany into
a realization that through her military policy, dictated by an autocratic group that cannot be called
to account by the people, Germany has become a
menace to the safety of the world. The German
army—in its origin the creation of the German
people organized to fight for its liberty as a nation—
has become a mighty weapon in the hands of the
rulers of Germany to hold the people at their mercy
and to use the splendid patriotism of the people (that
brought 1,800,000 volunteers to the front within
one week after the declaration war), for the furtherance of plans that endanger the happiness of
other nations and that are to serve towards strengthening the power of autocracy. This " new " Germany, revealed by the conduct of the war, must be
overcome in order to bring back the Germany of
ante-bellum days. The " old " Germany, we now
sadly recognize, died in 1914—possibly earlier, on
June 15, 1888, when Frederick III, surnamed the
" Noble," passed away after a reign of one hundred
days.[1] The old Germany, as Brandes well says,
gave us " everything German that is loved or appreciated." It can be recreated only through the democra-

---

[1] George Brandes, a friend and lover of Germany if ever
there was one, calls these one hundred days the " short gleam
of a clear human spirit breaking in on our war-mad empire."
The World at War, p. 6.

tization of Germany's form of government. This advance will assuredly come about either during the war, or as a direct result of the war, when the ghastly crisis through which the world is passing shall happily be a thing of the past, to become, after the lapse of some years, a memory that will continue to haunt the world for generations to come.

Unless, however, at the end of the war, the great nations of the world give the proper cue for the work of reconstruction by advocating a policy of *co-operation* with the East, instead of open or disguised exploitation, we will continue to have an Eastern Question that may again pass through the same process (with perhaps different contestants) to culminate in open hostility. "Internationalization" of all schemes for opening up the East to the West is the solution of the Eastern Question for which I have ventured to enter a plea at the close of this book.

It remains for me to make acknowledgment, as in the case of all my publications, to the invaluable assistance given to me by my dear wife in reading both the manuscript and the proof, and helping in various other ways, including the encouragement to trespass upon fields adjacent to my own and to which the study of the war in the East led me. I also wish to make grateful acknowledgment to my friend, Mrs. Gardiner Gayley, for many suggestions made in discussing with her the plan and the thesis of this study. To my former student, Hon. Edward I. Nathan, American Consul at Mersina from 1910 to the breaking of our diplomatic relations with Turkey, and who has rendered distinguished services at his responsible post, I am under obligations for criticisms and for valuable information regarding the industries of Turkey, par-

ticularly at Mersina, which I have embodied in
one of the notes attached to the volume. I should
like to call particular attention to these notes in
which I have given bibliographical and explanatory
details for those who wish to pursue the subject
further. The map, prepared by Mr. Earl Thatcher
with great care, will, I trust, prove useful. I am
indebted to Mr. Leon Dominian, of the American
Geographical Society, for permission to make use
of his map of railroads in Turkey published by him
in "Frontiers of Language and Nationality in
Europe" (Henry Holt & Co., N. Y., 1917). A special
feature of my map is the inclusion of all railroads,
both those constructed and those projected in Asia
Minor, Syria, Palestine and Mesopotamia. The
map will enable the reader to follow the further
course of development of the war in the various
sections of the Near East. For countries, lying outside of the special topic of this volume, I have contented
myself with indicating merely a few places as an orien-
tation; and in order not to confuse the reader by making
the map too crowded, I have selected for Asia Minor
only the important places and more particularly
those that are connected with events in the history
of the region. My thanks are due to Dr. Edward
Robinson, Director of the Metropolitan Museum of
New York, who kindly placed at my disposal a
photograph of the fine Hittite monument of the
Museum—the only one of the kind (so far as I am
aware) in this country. To my friend and colleague,
Professor J. H. Breasted, of the University of
Chicago, and to the publishers, Ginn & Co. and the
University of Chicago, I am indebted for permission
to use two illustrations, one in his excellent manual
on *Ancient History* (Boston, 1916) and the other
from his monograph, *The Battle of Kadesh* (Chicago,

1901); to Professor John Garstang for permission to use some of the illustrations in his *Land of the Hittites* (Dutton & Co., New York); to Mr. Ernest Leroux for the similar courtesy to use some illustrations from Nettancourt-Vaubecourt *Sur Les Grandes Routes de l'Asie Mineure* (Paris, 1908) published by him; and to Mr. C. E. Lydecker, the Counsellor of the American Chamber of Commerce of Constantinople, for his approval in using several illustrations from The Levant Trade Review—a most important source of information for the commerce and industries of the Near East, and to which I am particularly glad to call the attention of all interested in Eastern matters.

To the Hon. Otis A. Glazebrook, who has made such a notable record as United States Consul at Jerusalem till the diplomatic break with Turkey, I beg to make acknowledgment for authentic information in regard to present conditions of railways in Palestine.

Mr. H. De Wolf Fuller, the editor of *The Nation* (New York) has kindly permitted me to embody in this book, in an enlarged and revised form, some views set forth by me in an article written for *The Nation* and published in the issue of August 30, 1916, under the title of " The World's Highway." Lastly, it is a genuine pleasure to dedicate the little volume to the members of the Wednesday Morning Club, of Pittsfield (Mass.), in recollection of many visits to the charming " heart of the Berkshires " as their guest. To speak before the delightful and sympathetic audience that gathers at the weekly reunions of this Club during the summer months is a privilege which I am sure all who are invited to do so value as highly as I do.

MORRIS JASTROW, JR.

UNIVERSITY OF PENNSYLVANIA
   November, 1917

CONTENTS

ILLUSTRATIONS

THE WAR AND THE BAGDAD RAILWAY

CHAPTER I
THE WAR IN THE EAST

I

HISTORY is being made to-day through the war in lands replete with historic associations, that have witnessed the rise and decay of many a civilization. The conflict raging in three continents and shared in by the fourth sees armies taking possession of the valley of the Nile, whose pyramids were built 5000 years ago. Passing over a route identical in part with that of the traditional Exodus, the march of the English troops toward Jerusalem suggests a repetition of the Crusades of the Middle Ages. Cross and Crescent once more lock arms at sites that have acquired a sacred significance in the traditions of three religions. Further East, Russian armies are following the route of the Ten Thousand [1] on the eastern border of Asia Minor, and are moving in Persia along some of the old routes on which the hosts of Cyrus passed in their descent upon the Euphrates Valley, and which two centuries later witnessed the remarkable invasion of the old East

---

[1] Trebizond at the southeastern corner of the Black Sea, captured by the Russians in the early campaigns of the war, is the point where the Greeks on their retreat from Babylonia (401 B.C.) at last reached the seashore.

23

by the young Lochinvar, come out of the West. The imagination is stirred by the exploits of English armies landing at the head of the Persian Gulf and moving along the Tigris across the mounds, which have in part yielded but in large part still cover the remains of the civilization that arose in the Euphrates Valley thousands of years ago and which, spreading northwards, became the rival of Egyptian achievements.

Can any romance be stranger than the streets of Bagdad, only sixty miles distant from the ruins of ancient Babylon, with memories of past glory reaching back to Harun al-Rashid, resounding to the steps of European soldiery, and Mosul, opposite which lies all that remains of Nineveh " the great city," once mistress of the world, at the mercy of a European power! What does it all mean? It is reported that on the top of the remains of one of the ancient towers that formed a feature of the temples of Babylonia a " wireless " station has been installed since the beginning of the war. This particular tower is the one, curiously enough, which tradition associates with the famous Tower of Babel. Are we perhaps to see in the use to which this sentinel of a hoary antiquity has been converted an omen of the conquest of the East by the aggressive West? Or is it a symbol of the resuscitation of the East through the infusion of the progressive spirit of the West? Are the dry bones scattered through the valley as in the vision of Ezekiel,[2] once more to be knit together with sinews and to be covered with new flesh?

On the other hand, in Arabia the standard of re-

---

[2] Ezekiel, Chap. 37.

volt has been unfurled.[3] The cry has been raised
to reclaim the land in which Mohammed preached
his new religion in the early part of the seventh
century of our era for the people to which Mohammed belonged. Are we to witness perhaps a revival of the spirit which once created mighty forces
to spread the Koran with the help of the sword
throughout the world? Up to the present, to be
sure, the " revolt " in Arabia hardly merits so digni-
fied a name. The accounts of it sound more like a
score of opera bouffe than a serious performance,
but the anomaly presented for many centuries of a
religion so essentially a product of the Semitic mind
and an expression more particularly of the Arabic
spirit as Islam controlled by a power of non-Arabic
origin cannot endure for all times. To have the
Sheikh el-Islam, the " chief of the church," at Constantinople, merely because Constantinople became
the centre of a Turkish Empire four centuries ago,
and a purely nominal head at that under the sur-
veillance of a Young Turk cabinet, suspected of infi-
delity and acting at the dictation of German officials,
is indeed ludicrous. But England in encouraging
the demand of Arabia for the Arabs—for she is behind this revolt—may be stirring up a spirit which
it will be hard for her to control, for the spirit of
Islam is still the spirit of fanaticism that sees only
the doings of Iblis in a world that does not acknowledge Mohammed as the apostle of Allah. " Die ich
rief, die Geister, werd' ich nun nicht los," says
Goethe. The Near East is still largely the Moham-

[3] See Snouck Hurgronje's vivid account " The Revolt
in Arabia," with a foreword by Richard J. H. Gottheil (New
York, 1917).

medan East, capable of acting in accord if a great leader should arise, who will succeed in uniting the followers of Orthodox Sunna ("tradition") with the Shiites [4] for a great common cause. Islam does not spell Progress. If reinforced, it may lead to a revival of a Near East that will once more be the antagonist of western culture, rather than a minor partner. The revival of the East is thus fraught with various possibilities that may take a turn for good or evil according to the throw of the dice on the table of fate. Or shall we accept the more comforting western belief that we can control the dice, and by wise counsels direct the course of events into the right channels? Which shall it be, the optimistic creed of the West, "Life and death, the blessing and the curse, have I placed before thee, choose thou life" (Deuteronomy 30, 19), or the fatalism of the disillusioned East, which declares that "Allah is the only knowing one"?

II

THE key to the situation, however, lies not in Egypt nor in Arabia, neither in Palestine nor in Mesopotamia, but in the region of Asia Minor— along the great highway leading from Constantinople to Bagdad. That region has from the most ancient times determined the fate of the Near East. Its rôle in the distant past has ever been to threaten the existence of civilizations and powers that arose

---

[4] Islam, apart from numerous sects, is divided into two great divisions formed by those who follow the "sunna" or Orthodox tradition, as against those who set up the claim that Ali was the direct successor of Mohammed. The latter are known as "Shiites" ("partisans").

in the valley of the Nile and in the valley of the Euphrates, as in the intervening lands of Palestine and Arabia. Egypt, Babylonia and Assyria exhausted their vitality in warding off the menace of the hordes that held the region. Hebrew Prophets announced the doom of the world through the coming of nations from the north—meaning Asia Minor. Cyrus and Alexander began their conquests of the old-time world by first securing a grasp on Asia Minor. With that in their hands, Babylonia, Palestine and Egypt fell easily into their lap. The Romans kept their grasp on the East as long as they held the routes through the mountain ridges of central Asia Minor. Islam failed in its world conquest because it could not hold this wild region in check, and the union of the Arabs broke up into rival caliphates. Decisive battles of the Crusades took place along these historic routes. A kingdom of Jerusalem was destined to failure from the start because it lay exposed to attacks from the North. The Turkish Empire was founded with the conquest of Constantinople in 1453, because through that event the control of the highway leading to the Persian Gulf was established. As long as that empire was able to maintain the two poles of the electric wire stretching from Constantinople to Bagdad, her dominant position remained unchallenged; her definite decline begins with a break in the current.

The conquest of that highway by Ottoman Turks meant the final triumph of Crescent over Cross, for it erected a barrier, shutting off Christian Europe from access to the entire East. A new route to India had to be found, and so in 1492 Columbus, sailing from Spain with this end in view, discovered a new continent.

In our own days we are witnessing what promised to be the reopening of the old historic highway —the bridge uniting Europe to Asia—to Western control, through the project of a great railway stretching along a distance of nearly 2000 miles from a point opposite Constantinople to Bagdad, and thence to Basra and to the Persian Gulf. That project, which was well under way at the time of the outbreak of the war, is thus marked through its historical background as one of the most momentous enterprises of our age—more momentous because of the issue involved than the opening up of the two other world highways, the Suez and Panama canals.

The creation of a railway from Constantinople to Bagdad under European control is at once a symptom of the dissolution of the Turkish Empire which has become a mere shadow of its former wide extension, and a significant token of the new invasion of the East by the spirit of Western enterprise. Passing along a highway over which armies have marched forward and backward ever since the days of antiquity, the railway is also a link connecting the present with the remote past.

More than this a project, which, on the surface, would appear to be solely commercial, assumes a romantic aspect through the struggle that the railway aroused for the control of a region that marked the ambition of all the great empires of ancient and mediæval times. The rivalry between Germany, England, France and Russia, centering so largely during the past decade around the Bagdad Railway, is merely the renewal under changed conditions of a conflict that began thousands of years ago. The modern world fights for this region as the ancient world did, with the railroad as the new symbol of a possession stronger and firmer than the garrisons and outposts of antiquity and the fortresses of the Roman and mediæval periods. The importance of Constantinople lies in its position as the starting-point of the great highway that has as its natural outlets the Bay of Alexandretta on the one hand, and the Persian Gulf on the other. The historical rôle of this highway gives to the Bagdad Railway a political import far transcending its aspect as one of the great commercial enterprises of our days. Backed as the project was by the German government, steadily growing in power and aggressiveness since the establishment of the united German Empire, it added to the already complicated Eastern Question an aggravating factor that contributed largely to the outbreak of the great war. The present struggle for supremacy among European powers resolves itself in its ultimate analysis into a rivalry for the control of the East as an adjunct to commercial expansion. The "trend towards the East"[5] did not originate with modern Germany. It began with Greece, was taken up by ancient Rome and has actuated every Western power with ambitions to extend its commerce and its sphere of influence—Spain, Holland, England and France, and in days nearer to us Russia and Germany, Austria and Italy. Through a curious combination of circumstances, superinduced by the gradual weakening of the once dominant Turkish Em-

---

[5] "Drang nach Osten"—a favorite phrase among German political and economic publicists.

pire, the struggle has shaped itself into its present aspect for a control of the great highway that is the key to the East—the nearer and the farther East.

A survey of the history of Asia Minor, as a resultant of the geographical contour of the region, furnishes the illustration to the thesis that the most recent events are merely the repetition on a larger scale of such as took place thousands of years ago, and at frequent intervals since. The weapons have changed, new contestants have arisen to take the place of civilizations that after serving their day faded out of sight, but the issue has ever remained the same. We are confronted by that issue to-day —the control of the highway that leads to the East. Through the war archæological investigations and historical researches have been removed from their academic isolation to furnish the explanation for the political import of the Bagdad Railway project. The study of the remote past, so energetically pursued by European and American scholars during the past decades, is brought into the foreground through the stirring events of our days to illumine the bearings of the historic highway of Asia Minor on the issues at stake in the present world conflict. The decisive battlefields for the triumph of democracy are in the West, but the decision for supremacy among European nations lies in the East. The Bagdad Railway is the most recent act in a drama the beginnings of which lie in the remote past.

To understand the Bagdad Railway project, therefore, we must turn to the rôle that Asia Minor has played in history. That history reveals to us why Asia Minor was ever, in the past, as she is to-day, the determining element in bringing about the alternate rise and decline of the East.

CHAPTER II

THE STORY OF ASIA MINOR

I

ASIA MINOR is the *Hinterland* to Syria, Palestine and Egypt on the one side, and to Mesopotamia on the other. With an area of about 206,378 square miles [1] (a little larger than France and a little smaller than Germany) its distinctive features are (1) a series of high plateaus in the interior, sloping from 2000 feet at the western edge to over 4000 feet towards the eastern border, with (2) several mountain ranges traversing the region longitudinally, rising in the north to over 8000 feet and in the south to over 10,000 feet, (3) a deeply indented western coast line with a fringe of protecting islands and with deep gulfs affording plenty of harbors. In contrast, the bleak north coast on the Black Sea has few harbors and no islands, while the southern coast is marked by a broad bay and a deep gulf and a number of land-locked harbors. The rivers, though numerous, are of no great importance, and only a few are navigable for a short distance from their mouths. On the plateaus, broken by broad valleys in the west, the winters are long and cold, and the summers hot. The coast climate varies from cold winters and humid summer vegetation on the Black Sea to a moderate cli-

---

[1] Its greatest length is 720 miles along the northern edge and at the south edge 650 miles. The breadth varies from 300 to 420 miles.

mate on the west coast, the summer heat being tempered by an almost daily north wind blowing off the sea, and reaching to extreme summer heat and mild winters on the south coast. Along the course of the rivers, vegetation is rich, aided by alluvial deposits to the soil, brought down by the streams as they pass through mountain gorges. The mineral wealth of Asia Minor is very great, and it would appear that iron was introduced as early as the second millenium before our era into the ancient East, through the working of the ore in the north-eastern corner of Asia Minor.

The contrast presented by the coast land to that of the interior is paralleled by the totally different aspect of the earliest settlements along the Ægean Sea from the conditions that led to the rise of powerful states in the interior. The western coast of Asia Minor appears to have been settled in very early days through Ægean traders coming probably from Crete where, as the remarkable excavations of the last two decades have shown, a high degree of civilization, more commonly spoken of as Minoan, was developed between c. 3000 and 2500 B.C. It reached its height about 1600 B.C., but long ere this sent its offshoots to the Grecian mainland, notably to Argos. The great castles and palaces of Mycenæ and Tiryns, excavated by Schlieman, are the works of these Ægeans coming from Crete, and there are traces of such settlements and influences elsewhere. The proto-Greek civilization, commonly spoken of as Mycenean, thus turns out to be of Cretan origin. Similarly, these Ægeans came to the coast of Asia Minor, and in time a powerful kingdom with Troy

ENTRANCE OF THE FAMOUS CILICIAN GATES

VIEW NEAR SARDIS

as a centre was established in the northwestern corner, reaching its height between c. 1500 and 1200 B.C.[2] The Homeric poems, commemorating the conflicts between Ægeans and Greeks, are thus brought nearer to us by the spade of the archælogist. These Ægeans belonged to the Indo-European stock, and, in passing, it may be noted that the Philistines who as traders settled on the Palestinian coast (and gave their name to the country) also came from Crete, and represent, therefore, a part of a general movement of the spread of Ægean civilization, though confined to coast lands. Whether the earliest settlers of the interior of Asia Minor belonged to this same general stock, designated by the unsatisfactory term "Aryan," is not certain, though possible, but in any case these settlers appear to have come from the steppes of southern Russia across the Caucasus Mountains. From this centre streams of migration radiated in various directions, some passing to the southeast and eventually reaching India where they developed the old Hindu civilization; others passed around the Black Sea on the north and moved along the Danube into central Europe, and still others entered Asia Minor somewhere near its northeastern border. Traces of very ancient routes along this southern coast of the Black Sea and running into the interior [3] show how early the settlement of the interior of Asia Minor must have begun.

---

[2] The so-called sixth city of Schlieman's excavations. See Walter Leaf, *Troy*, pp. 85-101 and the map.

[3] See Ramsay's invaluable work, "The Historical Geography of Asia Minor" (London, 1890), chapters I-VII, for a full discussion of these old routes.

II

A region like the interior of Asia Minor broken up by mountain ranges, with no large river as an avenue of transportation, is not conducive to the creation of a single state, uniting groups of population through common interests. Rivalry rather than permanent union would represent the natural tendency among the combinations that would be formed by the hordes moving from time immemorial across the Caucasus and from lands lying beyond to the north and northeast. An indigenous civilization arising under such conditions would be marked by a hardiness reflecting the traits of the region. The break-up of the population through natural barriers separating the various groups would tend to the unfolding of strength, in order to secure protection from attack and to safeguard an independent existence. Such peoples will build huge fortified castles and will create strong armies, actuated by the natural ambition to put their strength to a test. Asia Minor is thus adapted to develop powers marked by militarism.

Excavation and exploration in the interior of Asia Minor during the last thirty years have, as a matter of fact, revealed the existence of powerful military states organized by groups known as Hittites, and whose history reverts to the border of the third millennium before this era. Until archæology had thus opened up the early history of Asia Minor, nothing was known of these Hittites beyond what could be gleaned from incidental notices in the Old Testament, where they appear chiefly as one of the groups like the Amorites, Perizzites and Canaanites

with whom the Hebrews were forbidden to marry.
Then, as Egyptian and Babylonian monuments re-
leased their secrets, references to the Khatti, whom
scholars at first hesitatingly identified with the
Hittites of the Old Testament, began to multiply in
the records of Egyptian and Assyrian rulers. Gradually, it became evident that these Hittites must have
been the most serious menace that the two great
civilizations of the Near East had to encounter.
Hittites loomed up larger and larger, as the written
and pictorial material increased, but the full force
of their position and achievements was not recognized until, through more thorough exploration,
Hittite monuments and Hittite remains turned up
in various parts of Asia Minor, dating back to the
second millennium before this era.

The character of these monuments and remains
scattered throughout Asia Minor and northern Syria
is so marked that there can be no doubt of their
belonging to the same civilization. Rock sculptures,
stone reliefs and inscribed stones extend east to west
from Sipylos, not far from Smyrna, to Malatia on the
Euphrates, and north to south from Boghaz-
Keui to Hama on the Orontes, all showing the
same characteristics. Great fortresses and palaces
of elaborate construction have been found at Boghaz-
Keui and Eyuk in northern Asia Minor and in Sakje-
Geuzi and Sendjerli in the southeast beyond the
Taurus range. These sites represent some of the
walled towns of the Hittites, of which there were
many, scattered throughout the region at strategical
points near the mountain passes and elsewhere along
the main routes. The scale of the constructions and
of the rock sculptures illustrate the power developed

by the Hittites in the hey-day of their glory, which
extends from c. 1500 to 1000 B.C. The entrance to
the fort was through enormous gates flanked by lions
or sphinxes. The city walls and the defences were
constructed of large stones built in the most solid
masonry. At Eyuk, some 20 miles to the north
of Boghaz-Keui, on either side of the gateway, there
is a long series of huge blocks on which scenes of a
religious character, processions of priests and musi-
cians, paying homage to a god and goddess, were
sculptured in relief. Elsewhere the rocks portray vivid
scenes of stag and lion hunts which were favorite sports
of the Hittite rulers.

Finally, there are a large number of inscriptions
in the peculiar Hittite hieroglyphic characters,
accompanying the sculptures, and the many inscribed stones containing the explanation of the
scenes or embodying votive dedications. By the side
of these inscribed lapidary monuments, excavations
at Boghaz-Keui conducted by the late Hugo Winckler in 1906–1907 have brought to light, to cap the
surprise of scholars, thousands of clay tablets, like
those found in Babylonian and Assyrian mounds,
covered with cuneiform characters, but representing
not the Sumerian (non-Semitic) or Akkadian (Semitic) language of the Euphrates Valley, but Hittite—
the same language as that of the hieroglyphic inscriptions, transliterated into cuneiform.[4] This proof of
the adoption of the cuneiform script for writing
Hittite, because more convenient and simpler for
correspondence and business documents—and that

---

[4] A parallel would be to come across Egyptian inscriptions
written not with any of the varieties of the Egyptian script,
but with Greek letters.

HITTITE ROCK SCULPTURE AT IVRIZ (C. 1000 B.C.)

RUINS OF THE ENTRANCE TO A HITTITE FORTRESS AT
BOGHAZKEUI (C. 1500 B.C.)

as early at least as 1500 B.C—is one of the most notable results of archæological activity in Asia Minor. It points to the intercourse that must have existed between Asia Minor and the Euphrates Valley in the second millenium before this era.

Although the Hittite hieroglyphics have not as yet been deciphered, the character of the language spoken by the Hittites has been established. It turns out to belong to the "Aryan" or more properly the Indo-European stock—a somewhat surprising discovery, and yet in keeping with the most plausible hypothesis of the origin of the Hittites from the steppes of southern Russia as the starting-point of successive waves of Aryan migration in various directions.

Looking, however, at the types of Hittite as pictured on their sculptures, one cannot escape the comparison with Mongoloid types, and this impression is confirmed by the representation of Hittites on Egyptian monuments which give us distinctly the high cheek-bones and retreating forehead, characteristic of the Tartar races. To these features is to be added the pig-tail,[5] depicted on Egyptian monuments and so consistently portrayed on Hittite sculptures. By the side of this type, however, we find also on the Egyptian monuments, portraying scenes and expeditions in Asia Minor, another which is more Indo-European in character, and we encounter this type also in some of the figures in the religious processions and in the ceremonial designs on tombstones throughout the Hittite region. Such indications point again to the supposition which, on

---

[5] The pig-tail is, however, not confined to the Tartars and Chinese.

a priori grounds, is plausible that what we call the Hittite civilization is the result of a commingling of different ethnic groups. Culture seems to be the spark that ensues when two different elements meet and combine, though in time one of the elements predominates.

III

It will be evident from this survey that the term Hittite is to be regarded as a very general one to mark a type of civilization in which the Hittite became the *predominating* element, but in which, as a product of the mixture of Hittites with other ethnic elements, others than Hittites participate. It is natural, therefore, to find various centres of Hittite culture. We find several Hittite states of considerable power in northern Syria, while further north, Boghaz-Keui became the capital of a Hittite state, which in the middle of the fifteenth century B.C. acquired a commanding position over a large part of Asia Minor, including northern Syria.

Now the historical significance of these Hittite states lies entirely in their geographical position, which made them a menace to Egypt on the one hand and to Babylonia on the other, while Palestine as the unfortunate buffer state between these two civilizations was even more at the mercy of the warlike Hittites. The early history of Asia Minor is linked to the fortunes of these three lands. The key to the understanding of the political development of the ancient East, accompanying the rise of a high order of civilization in the two fertile valleys—the Nile and the Euphrates—lies in an appreciation of the fact that Egypt and Babylonia could only maintain themselves by successfully holding in check the rugged mountaineers of Asia Minor. Attracted by the allurements of a far higher culture than their own, the Hittites would be tempted, as their strength increased to break through their natural barriers and to seek the plains of Mesopotamia and the lowlands of Egypt, with Palestine as a natural passageway too insignificant ever to unfold any considerable power of her own. Once the mountain passes of the Anti-Taurus and Amanus ranges were crossed, there was nothing to prevent the rugged mountaineer forces from marching along to the Mediterranean coast, to Palestine and Egypt, or eastwards to the Euphrates—the avenue to both Babylonia in the south and to Assyria towards the north. Assyria could also be reached by direct routes from eastern Asia Minor, following river courses and through mountain passes to Diarbekr and thence along the Tigris. That this was the actual part played by the Hittite groups from very early days down to their final dissolution at the close of the eighth century before this era, when new forces made their appearance in Asia Minor, is shown by Egyptian and Babylonian and Assyrian records stretching from before 2000 B.C. to the fall of Assyria herself in 606 B.C.

It is surprising to find that as early as 1900 B.C. Hittites actually invaded the Euphrates Valley. We have the official record of a Hittite occupying at this time the throne of Babylon. The Hittite occupation did not last long, but the fact of its having been accomplished for a short period shows the power which these doughty warriors must have acquired by the beginning of the second millenium. The danger of an attack from the region to the north and north-west of the Euphrates Valley must have been real-

ized by the Babylonian rulers, for we find them
establishing an outpost against the Hittites as early
as 2400 B.C. beyond the Anti-Taurus range in what is
now known as Cappadocia. On this supposition we
can account for the discovery of numerous cuneiform
tablets near Cæsarea. The contents of these tablets
are of a business nature. They deal with commercial transactions, and the language is a kind of
patois, Babylonian mixed with foreign words that
will probably turn out to be Hittite. Since they
are dated after the fashion of Babylonian documents,
we are in a position to determine their age as ranging
from about 2400 to 2000 B.C. The proof which they
furnish of active business transactions between the
Euphrates Valley and Asia Minor is of the greatest
value in illustration of trade routes that must have
been established through the heart of Asia Minor
at this early period. Trade and war are close bed-
fellows in antiquity, as they are in modern days.
Trade in this instance must have been incidental to
the garrison established by Babylonian rulers at a
strategic point far north, to ward off an advance
of Hittites across the mountain passes of the Anti-
Taurus and the Amanus ranges in the direction of
the Euphrates Valley—precisely the menace that
overwhelmed the Euphrates Valley some centuries
later. The Euphrates Valley could not be held without the *Hinterland,* which in itself is the continuation
of the " Fertile Crescent " that starts at the Persian
Gulf and stretches in a semi-circle around a desert
region to the Mediterranean. We accordingly find
a great conqueror like Sargon I (c. 2700 B.C.), under
whom the Akkadians (or Semites) gain their first definite triumph over the Sumerians, leading his armies

AN ANCIENT HITTITE AND HIS
MODERN ARMENIAN DESCENDANT

MONOLITH OF A HITTITE RULER WITH INSCRIPTION
(METROPOLITAN MUSEUM)

northward and obtaining a firm hold to the shores of the Mediterranean. Sargon's predecessors were satisfied with being kings of Sumer and Akkad,[6] comprising the Euphrates Valley, but he and his successors aspire to the grandiloquent title of "King of the Four Regions." It was, however, military necessity rather than an original greed of conquest that led these early rulers to become conquerors and to convert their empire into a military power.

Under such conditions, the destiny of Babylonia lay inevitably in the direction of becoming a strong military state, with its chief aim to secure control of as large a territory as possible to the north and northwest, so as to maintain itself against encroachments of Hittite groups from these directions. When Babylonia waxed strong, the Hittites were kept in suppression, when it grew weaker, we find the Hittites acquiring greater strength. A period of decline set in in the Euphrates Valley at the end of the eighteenth century, when the control passes for five centuries into the hands of a people known as the Cassites and whose origin is still doubtful.

The weakness of Babylonia furnishes the favorable opportunity for the unfolding of greater strength in Assyria to the north. The admixture of Hittite elements in the population of Assyria stamped Assyria as more naturally warlike from the start than Babylonia, but her rulers likewise had to fortify themselves against invasions from Asia Minor along routes that led along the eastern extremity of that region, identical in part with the march of the Rus-

---

[6] Sumer is the designation of the southern part of the Valley, Akkad, to which the Semitic settlers were driven back by the Sumerians, the designation of the northern part.

sian army in the present war from Trebizond to
Erzerum southwards in the direction of Mosul—
opposite which lay Nineveh, the later capital of
Assyria, and a little to the south Ashur, the older
capital.   Assyria was unable, however, to prevent
the rise of a powerful Hittite kingdom in northern
Asia Minor with its centre at Boghaz-Keui, c. 1500
B.C., and which succeeded in obtaining a dominant
position over Hittite centres and settlements throughout eastern and central Asia Minor and beyond the
Anti-Taurus range in northern Syria, close to the
borders of Mesopotamia.

IV

Turning to Egypt, we find this region during the
first period of her most ancient history, the so-called
Pyramid Age, extending from about 3000 to 2500
B.C., marked by high achievements in art, notably the
building of the great pyramids on the outskirts of the
capital, Memphis.   Egypt like Babylonia was a cultural
power, and as such advanced through peaceable progress rather than by the force of arms.   Civilizations
that arise in valleys and in islands do not develop
military strength, except for purposes of defence;
they are essentially pacific.   The centre of the Egyptian kingdom was in the north.   There were, to be
sure, encounters with the south, as a natural result
of the extension of Egyptian culture, but there were
no attempts at conquest beyond the natural borders.
It was not till the close of the Feudal Age (c. 2500 to
1800 B.C.), that we find standing armies organized,
though on a moderate scale, with the help of which
Nubia was conquered and Palestine, as the coastland
immediately adjoining Egypt and a natural bulwark,

brought under the control of the Pharaohs. An entirely different aspect is assumed by Egyptian history with a new line of rulers, marked by extraordinary energy, who come upon the scene about 1600 B.C. A new capital is established at Thebes, about 400 miles to the south of Memphis. The change is significant as indicative of the larger extent of the empire, which brought with it a transfer of the seat of government nearer to the centre of the dominion. No doubt a contributing factor also in the change was the need of a powerful bulwark closer to the southern frontier, which at all times needed to be protected against attacks from the population in central Africa. What led to the decline of the Pharaohs of the Feudal Age, so named because of the position which the nobles, owning large estates under royal agents, acquired, is still a mystery. The age was marked by progress in literature, leading to collections of papyrus rolls that assumed the dimensions of libraries, as well as by an advance in ethical standards. Was it perhaps a long period of intellectual development that softened the virile qualities of the Egyptians so that they fell an easy prey to foreigners who seized the throne?

These are the so-called Hyksos or "shepherd" kings, a traditional designation whose identification is still a matter of dispute among Egyptologists. The designation points to an identification of these invaders with the Semitic nomads from Arabia and Palestine who at frequent intervals passed into Egypt, attracted by the higher civilization, just as the Euphrates Valley proved a magnet for Bedouin groups coming into Babylonia by way of the Euphrates. The movement of some of the Hebrew groups into

Egypt as depicted by the traditional narratives of Genesis furnishes an illustration of such an invasion. prompted in part also by economic conditions. Large settlements of these Semitic nomads were made in the outlying districts of Egypt bordering on and near the Red Sea. It is, however, on the face improbable that such loosely organized bands, not particularly warlike and occupying a grade of culture only some degrees removed from primitive conditions, should have been capable of taking hold of the government of Egypt. Some stronger factor must be assumed that may have utilized these nomads in a serious attack on Egypt. Recalling that as early as 1900 B.C. the Hittites invaded Babylonia, and that Biblical tradition reports the presence of Hittites in southern Palestine at this same early date, it is a reasonable conjecture that the leaders of the invasion were the powerful Hittites, who in alliance with the nomads wrested the throne of Egypt from the native rulers and occupied it for a time until they were once more replaced by a native dynasty.[7]

However this may be, we soon find the Pharaohs of the new empire turning their faces in the direction of Asia, and under Thutmose III (c. 1500–1450 B.C.) these efforts at bringing Palestine and the Mediterranean coast and northern Syria well into the interior of Asia Minor under subjection reached their culmination. The motive, however, which originally prompted this military policy, was not greed of conquest but the necessity of maintaining the Egyptian empire unimpaired in her strength— the same condition, therefore, that changed Baby-

---

[7] See Garstang, *Land of the Hittites,* p. 324, who agrees in associating the Hyksos with Hittite influences.

Ionia from a naturally pacific to a military power. The land of the Nile could not be held without keeping in check the constant menace of an invasion from the north. The coast cities along the Mediterranean and the interior of Palestine had to be converted into Egyptian garrisons under the control of governors subject to the Pharaohs. Palestine and Syria thus became vassal states of Egypt, and this step was necessarily followed by an extension of military activities northward and eastward into the strongholds of the Hittites. Success brought with it the enlargement of ambitions, and under Thutmose III Egypt definitely enters upon a career of military conquest.

It is not accidental that this new epoch of military activity in Egyptian history is coincident with the period when the Hittites reached the height of their power under the kingdom which had its centre in Boghaz-Keui. The great strength developed by the Hittites had to be counterbalanced by the putting forth of the strongest effort on the part of Egypt. This was all the more important because Babylonia under the rule of the Cassites was unable to hold the Hittites in check, and Assyria in the north had not developed sufficient strength to do so. In the century following upon Thutmose III, we find Assyrian kings taking up the challenge and Shalmaneser I succeeds (c. 1300 B.C.) in sweeping the Hittites back from the Euphrates. In this period we encounter also the first alliances between Egypt and Babylonia, reinforced by intermarriages between the two courts, in order to present a united front against the Hittite forces.

The reign of Amenhotep IV, or Ikhnaton, famous in Egyptian history as a religious reformer, gave the

Hittites a breathing spell, for this remarkable ruler was more interested in reforms of the cult, in the encouragement of the new art,[8] and in other internal problems than in extending the sway of Egypt. A new line of kings succeeded Ikhnaton that took up the former military policy, and under Rameses II the crisis in the test of strength with the Hittites came. The Hittite ruler Mursil and the Egyptian Pharaoh locked arms at Kadesh on the Orontes (c. 1295 B.C.). The battle proved to be one of the decisive events in ancient history. All portions of Asia Minor were represented in the tremendous force that Mursil had gathered for the encounter. Rameses II, who gives us a detailed account of the battle, illustrated by numerous pictured representations, on the temple walls at Abu Simbel, at Abydos, at Luxor and Karnak, recounts how at first the battle went favorably for the Hittites. The king confesses that at one stage in the encounter he was in danger of being captured. In the end, however, the Egyptians secured the advantage and, if we may trust the Egyptian chronicler, the Hittites were driven off the field. Had the fortune of battle gone against the Egyptians, a Hittite invasion of Egypt would have been inevitable and the course of Egyptian history would have been radically changed. As it was, the battle of Kadesh merely marked the zenith of Hittite power, and Egypt could hereafter breathe more freely. Her safety, however, was always dependent upon her holding as a minimum foreign possession southern Syria to act as a bulwark against Hittite advance. The Hittites under Mursil again undertook an offensive against Egypt, aided by

---

[8] See on this reformer the note on p. 156.

THE BATTLE OF KADESH BETWEEN THE EGYPTIANS AND HITTITES (c. 1295 B.C.)

Amorites and other groups of Palestine. The tide
of war flowed and ebbed until c. 1280 B.C., when an
offensive and defensive treaty between Hattusil, the
Hittite ruler of Boghaz-Keui, and Rameses II was
drawn up, of which by a fortunate chance we now have
both the Egyptian and the Hittite accounts. On the
temple walls of Karnak Rameses records the fact of the
reception of the Hittite treaty sent by Hattusil on a
silver tablet. Some years later, c. 1266 B.C., to further
mark the friendship now existing between the two
empires, a Hittite princess was added to the harem
of Rameses. She was escorted to Egypt by her
royal father, accompanied by a retinue worthy of so
extraordinary an occasion. Thus Hittites and
Egyptians actually met in the Valley of the Nile.

One is reminded of the jealousies and suspicions
of modern powers when one reads on cuneiform
documents of an inquiry directed by the king of
Babylonia to Hattusil as to the meaning of this
alliance between Egyptians and Hittites. Was this
ancient " Entente Cordiale " aimed against the Babylonian Empire? Hattusil's answer is as diplomati-
cally correct and non-committal as possible. " The
King of Egypt and I have made an alliance and have
become brothers. Brothers we are and will be
against any common enemy." The implication,
however, is clear, and Hattusil made use of the situation to exert pressure upon Babylonia. Thus the
game of diplomacy was played thousands of
years ago.

The power of Egypt declined with the end of the
nineteenth dynasty at the turn of the thirteenth century. The succeeding dynasties were occupied with
protecting themselves against encroachments from

the south.   Even their hold on Palestine and the
Phœnician coast was relaxed so as to permit of the
establishment of an independent state by the
Hebrews in the interior, and by the Philistines and
Phœnicians on the coast.   We hear no more of
Egyptian encounters with Hittites to whom freer
scope was thus given by the decline of the military
strength of the Empire of the Nile.

A steady stream of hordes passing into Asia
Minor brought new groups into the fields that established independent states in the mountain recesses
and beyond in northern Syria.   These come into conflict more particularly with Assyria, whose rulers
from the twelfth century on find themselves obliged
to undertake expedition after expedition against one
group or the other.   Now it is a group known as the
Muski who hold a dominant position over the southern portions of Asia Minor, now the Phrygian Kingdom, founded probably by " Ægeans " who passed
into the interior during the period of Hittite decline
and who dominated a large portion of the western plateau, and some centuries later, newcomers
across the Caucasus, known as the Cimmerians, who
overran Asia Minor and put an end to Phrygian
independence, and against whom the Assyrian rulers
were obliged to lead their forces in order to maintain
their own position.   Tiglathpileser I (c. 1130–1100
B.C.) of Assyria is one of the names that looms up
large in this effort to keep the hordes and groups
of Asia Minor in check, but though successful in
part, his successors are unable to prevent the rise
of a powerful Hittite state in northern Syria with
Carchemish on the Euphrates as the centre, that
maintains itself till 717 B.C. when it is finally over-

come by Sargon II of Assyria. With this decisive event, the way was open to Assyria for the complete control of the lands around the Mediterranean. Palestine, the Phœnician coast, northern Arabia and Egypt fall into Assyria's hands. Ashurbanapal, the "Grande Monarque" of Assyria (668–626 B.C.), under whom the Assyrian Empire reaches its climax, receives the homage of the Lydians, who had established an independent kingdom in Asia Minor after the overthrow of the Hittites and the Phrygians. The removal of the Asia Minor menace was the condition needed to make Nineveh the mistress of the ancient world.

V

The earliest history of Asia Minor thus foreshadows the rôle which the control of the highway leading from Constantinople to Bagdad was destined to play in subsequent ages down to our own days. Asia Minor as the *Hinterland* to Egypt and Mesopotamia forced these empires to become military powers in order to secure their position against attacks from the north to which they were exposed, though what was originally a matter of necessity became through the allurements of conquest a growing ambition. *L'appétit vient en mangeant.*

The position of Babylon, as the capital of the united Euphrates states, on the Euphrates, at a point where it runs closest to the Tigris, was chosen because the Euphrates was the natural avenue along which the hordes of Asia Minor after having passed through the Cilician gates and the Amanus range would swoop down upon the Mesopotamian plain. The continuity of the historical relationship of Mesopotamia to Asia Minor is well illustrated by the per-

4

sistency of the site, constituting the natural centre of the Euphrates Valley. Seleucia (founded by Seleucus I in 312 B.C.), the capital in the days of Greek occupancy, Ctesiphon in the later Parthian period (founded c. 129 B.C.) and Bagdad in Arabian times (founded about 763 A.D.) are all within seventy miles from Babylon. The only significant change brought about by time and different circumstances is the transfer of the capital of the region from the banks of the Euphrates to that of the Tigris.[9] This was due to the growth of commerce which made for a position on the Tigris as the avenue of commerce [10] from the Persian Gulf up to the northern confines of Assyria. Seleucia was selected as the most favorable site on the Tigris, where that river runs closest to the Euphrates, so that the capital might serve the same purpose as ancient Babylon did in being at a strategic point to ward off an attack from Asia Minor, while the change from Seleucia to Bagdad—only 15 miles apart—appears to have been due to a deviation in the course of the Euphrates which brought it nearest to the Tigris, at some remove from Seleucia. The choice of Nineveh as the capital of Assyria was similarly dictated by strategic considerations to offset the Asia Minor menace.[11]

---

[9] Seleucia, 50 miles north of Babylon, lies on the western bank of the Tigris, Ctesiphon directly opposite on the eastern bank, and Bagdad, 15 miles further north, originally on the western bank, but now and for centuries chiefly on the eastern bank.

[10] The Euphrates is only navigable in parts, and as it approaches the Persian Gulf loses itself in swamp and marshes.

[11] The older capital at Ashur (represented by the mound Kaleh Shergat) is only some 40 miles further south.

It lay at the northern limit of navigation on the Tigris, which forms the avenue of approach to Mesopotamia from the eastern end of Asia Minor along the routes from Sinope and Trebizond that converge at Diarbekr, near the source of both the Tigris and Euphrates. For Assyria, lying to the north at the outskirts of the Anti-Taurus range, the danger lay in a direct attack from the region of Diarbekr. We find the Assyrian rulers establishing an outpost at or near this point, and placing monuments of themselves there with records of their achievements, in order to inspire terror among their inveterate enemies in the strongholds of northern and eastern Asia Minor. The history of Babylonia and Assyria thus moves along the centuries under the shadow of this menace from Asia Minor.

For Egypt, the possession of Palestine formed the natural bulwark against the north. We have seen that already towards the close of the Feudal Age, efforts were directed towards this end which culminated in the fifteenth century B.C., in placing officials under Egyptian suzerainty in the important towns of Palestine, Gaza, Byblos, Sidon and Jerusalem. All these towns attain their rank because of their strategic location. In the reports which these governors send to the Pharaohs of existing conditions, the Hittites are portrayed threatening the Egyptian control of Palestine and the coast. These troublesome groups appear to have overrun Palestine, coming down from their mountain strongholds across the great highway of Asia Minor that led to the plains of northern Syria through the passage of the Cilician gates. They intermingle freely with the native population—with the Amorites in the

north, and with the Canaanitish settlers and the
semi-nomadic groups further south. The Hebrew
tradition of Hittites as far south as Hebron [12] at the
time when the Hebrews first make their appearance
in the land reflects this state of affairs. The same
tradition represents Esau as marrying Hittite
women.[13] True to their warlike character, we find
Hittites forming a contingent in the Hebrew armies
of later days. Hebrew chroniclers take it as perfectly natural that among David's followers there
should be Hittites, like Ahimelech [14] and the unfortunate Uriah,[15] whose wife Bathsheba arouses
David's passion and on whom the king practises
a dastardly deception in order to secure possession of the woman. Solomon, the offspring of the
marriage, may thus himself have been half-Hittite.
This close association between Hebrew and Hittites,
as also with the Amorites, must have continued on
a considerable scale so that centuries afterwards the
prophet Ezekiel, rebuking the people for their
boasted superiority, could say of Jerusalem " the
Amorite was thy father and the Hittite thy mother." [16]
Biblical writers find it necessary to issue a warning
against intermarriages with Hittites.[17] In the enu-
meration of the nations of Palestine whom the
Hebrews found in possession, whom they are called
upon to exterminate, but whom they never suc-

---

[12] See note to p. 52 at the end of the volume.

[13] Genesis 26, 34.

[14] I Samuel 26, 6. It is presumably his son Abiathar,
who is one of David's priests (I Samuel 30, 7).

[15] II Samuel, Chapters 11-12.

[16] Ezekiel, 16, 3.

[17] Deuteronomy, 7, 3.

ceeded in entirely driving out, the Hittites are invariably included. The Jebusites who hold the heights of Jerusalem till the days of David appear to have been Hittites; and it is significant that the rise of the Hebrews to power under David and Solomon (c. 1000–950 B.C.) coincides with the decline of Hittite power in Asia Minor through the constant encounters with the well-organized armies of the Assyrians. While still maintaining their independent existence for another two cenuries, they were no longer strong enough to take the offensive nor to prevent other hordes from passing into Asia Minor, and so the opportunity came for the Hebrews to create a kingdom out of tribes that had hitherto been joined in a loose confederacy.

VI

Passing down the ages we find the Assyrian power, exhausted by incessant warfare, succumbing to a combination formed against her by Asia Minor hordes, abetted by Babylonia, that saw in the downfall of Assyria the possibility of a renewal of her own independence. Nineveh fell in 606 B.C. and the Neo-Babylonian Empire enjoyed a short but illustrious respite. Nebopolassar (625–604 B.C.) who begins his career as a governor of Babylonia under Assyrian suzerainty, makes himself independent and hands the throne to his son, the famous Nebuchadnezzar (604–561 B.C.) who is fired with the ambition to make himself, in imitation of the Assyrian rulers, the master of the ancient world. Less than forty years after Nebuchadnezzar's death, however, a new aspirant to world-conquest appears

in Cyrus who, coming from Persia, puts an end to
the Neo-Babylonian kingdom in 539 B.C.

It is significant that Cyrus begins his career by
an expedition to Asia Minor. The powerful kingdom in the sixth century in that region was Lydia,
which succeeded to Phrygia and held a considerable
part of Asia Minor. The final overthrow of the
Hittites by Sargon at the close of the eighth century gave the opportunity for other groups to secure
a dominant position in Asia Minor. The Lydians
were an Aryan people and possibly, like the Phrygians allied to the Ægeans, some of whom appear
to have passed inwards from the coast. Cyrus,
with the instinct of a great general, realizes that the
conquest of the *Hinterland* was a necessary condition to the establishment of an empire in the East.
Accordingly, he proceeds to Asia Minor and obtains
the supremacy over this region by the defeat of
Croesus, King of Lydia, in 546 B.C. His armies pass
over the historic highway through the Cilician gates,
along which Ashurbanapal had led his soldiers.
With this highway safely secured, he has no difficulty
in conquering Babylonia, which indeed yields to him
without a struggle in 539 B.C. Palestine also falls
into his hands, and his successor Cambyses passes
on in triumph to Egypt. The whole ancient world,
or at least all of it that seemed worth holding, falls
at the feet of the Persian rulers who pass from the
interior of Asia Minor to the coast and cross over
to Greece, besides taking possession of important
islands of the Ægean Sea like Cyprus. At the end
of the following century (401 B.C.) the younger
Cyrus, son of Darius II, likewise passes through
Asia Minor and seizes the Cilician gates as a pre-

liminary to an attempt to wrest the empire of the east from out of the hands of his elder brother Artaxerxes II. Cyrus was slain in the battle of Cunaxa, on the Euphrates, and soon thereafter the famous retreat of the " Ten Thousand " Greeks in the army of Cyrus through Asia Minor begins, to end successfully, after many hardships, at Trebizond on the Black Sea.

VII

Two centuries later the Persian Empire is threatened by a new force which likewise advances from the north. A new epoch in the world's history begins with the exploits of Alexander the Great (334–323 B.C.), who, after subduing Greece, begins his eastern campaigns at the northwestern corner of Asia Minor. On the river Granicus he defeats the Persian army that attempted to impede his passage. He passes along the same historic highway, on a route largely identical with the course of the Bagdad Railway, and emerging through the Cilician gates encounters the vast force which Darius had gathered at Issus. There he wins one of the decisive battles of the world's history. Master of Asia Minor, Alexander repeats the exploits of his Persian predecessors. Palestine and Egypt acknowledge his rule. He passes on to Mesopotamia, and after another sharp and victorious encounter with an army of Darius at Arbela, not far from Nineveh, the land of Assyria and Babylonia is added to his Empire.

The possession of Asia Minor is also the key to India. Alexander, whose ambition passes beyond the dreams of former conquerors, marches on to the river Indus, and is only checked in his progress by the opposition of his troops against a further advance. Still occupied with schemes of further conquest, he dies in Babylon by a strange fate in the huge palace which Nebuchadnezzar had erected for himself, with its terraced gardens, giving the impression of "hanging gardens," that were hailed as one of the wonders of the age.

Dissensions that broke out among Alexander's generals after his death led to a division of the vast empire. Seleucus (323–281 B.C.), who obtained Mesopotamia as his share, succeeded in bringing under his authority the entire eastern part of Alexander's Empire as far as the Jaxartes and Indus. It was evident, however, that Seleucus could not hold Mesopotamia without the *Hinterland* to the north and northwest, and so we find him and his successors striving for the possession of Asia Minor. At Ipsus in Asia Minor a decisive victory is won by Seleucus in 301 over his antagonist Antigonus, and with the *Hinterland* sufficiently secured to prevent an attack from this region, Syria and eventually Palestine and the coast towns fall under the Seleucid dynasty. Yet it was again from the north that the dominions of the Seleucids were threatened. In 278 B.C. the Gauls breaking into Asia Minor menaced the "Fertile Crescent," as the Hittites had done in their day. Antiochus I successfully blocked their advance and won for himself the title of *soter, i.e.,* "savior." It is significant that by driving the enemy out of Asia Minor, he is supposed to have saved the East. In the division of Alexander's conquests Egypt fell to the share of Ptolemy (323–283 B.C.) and a rivalry naturally ensued between the Ptolemies and the Seleucids. The former felt the need of holding Palestine as a bulwark, precisely as in the days of the Pharaohs, while the latter could content themselves generally, though not always, with acting on the defensive against Egypt, with the northern and eastern part of the " Fertile Crescent" in their control, backed by the *Hinterland*. Palestine became a ball tossed now to the Ptolemies, now to the Seleucids, until in the days of Antiochus III, sur-named the Great (223–187 B.C.), the Seleucids se-cured a more permanent possession of it, and proceed to the invasion of Egypt. The reign of this Antiochus represents both the climax of the Seleucid dynasty and the beginning of its decline. Once more the die is cast in Asia Minor. This region had been lost to the Seleucids in the reign of Seleucid II (246–227 B.C.), partly through internal dissension, and in part through the rise to power of the Pergamon Kingdom in the northwestern part of Asia Minor and which under its ruler, Attalus I (241–197 B.C.), had become a formidable rival.

The decline of Greek rule in the East thus begins with the loosening of the hold upon Asia Minor, as illustrated more particularly by the rise of the Per-gamon Kingdom. The Romans with a shrewd recognition of the importance of obtaining a foot-hold in Asia Minor as the starting-point for the development of a *Provincia Asia* allied themselves with the new kingdom. Through this Roman policy, the rulers of Pergamon added to their dominions most of western and a part of central Asia Minor.[18] The capital, Pergamon, became one of the most magnificent cities of the East, but only to fall into the hands of the Romans on the death of Attalus III

[18] Phrygia, Lydia, Pisidia, Lycaonia and Pamphylia become subject to Pergamon.

in 133 B.C. This marks the advent of Roman supremacy in the East. Pergamon retained its position
for a long time as the focusing point of military and
commercial routes of Asia Minor, traces of which
are still to be seen. From holding western Asia
Minor, Roman domination gradually spread until
under Pompey (64 B.C.) the entire region became subject to Rome, though certain provinces were permitted
to retain a nominal independence.

Since Alexander's days, however, Asia Minor had
become thoroughly Hellenized through the infusion
of Greek civilization. So strong was this impress
as to efface the traces of the old Hittite culture
completely. Only the ruins of buildings and the
rock sculptures remained to tell the tale of the earlier
days. Roman influence is to be seen in the building
and improvement of new roads through the country,
and in the erection of aqueducts as well as of garrisons with strong fortifications at strategic points.
The Greek spirit made for culture, the Roman for the
unfolding of strength, but through both commerce
was encouraged and followed in the wake of the
Greek and Roman occupation. Greek settlements
in Asia Minor can be followed by traces of the theatre
which formed a focus of Greek intellectual life. The
Romans, true to their genius, added the amphi-
theatre for gladitorial contests of strength.

VIII

Holding Asia Minor firmly, Rome fell heir to the
ancient civilizations of Egypt, Palestine and Mesopotamia. Until the end of the sixth century she
remained the undisputed mistress of the East. Her
weakness began to show itself, however, by the
increasing difficulties she encountered in holding the

pole at the one end of the historic highway—at the
Persian Gulf. She reversed the position that had
hitherto prevailed, for the Persians strongly entrenched at the southern end of the highway, stretching from Constantinople to the Persian Gulf, were
weak in their hold of the northern end. A general
of Darius Hystaspes held Byzantium for a while,
but the Greeks succeeded, c. 478 B.C., in regaining a
hold on the important site, the foundation of which
goes back to the seventh century B.C. During Greek
supremacy of the East, the same conditions prevailed. The Seleucidian rulers were always strong
in their control of the region of the Persian Gulf,
but weakest in their hold of the other pole. Following the example set by Alexander, his successors
devoted themselves to the maintenance of the network of canals of the Euphrates and Tigris, which
constituted one of the greatest achievements of the
older rulers of Babylonia.

Babylonia is the gift of the two rivers of Mesopotamia, as Egypt is the gift of the Nile. In both
regions a high order of civilization developed as a
result of the favorable conditions under which agri-
culture could be carried on in lowlands through
artificial irrigation. The partnership between nature
and man thus produced the culture and wealth
of Mesopotamia. Nature provided the soil, man
directed the outflow of the rivers through canals and
irrigation ditches into the fields, changing the curse
of an annual deluge into the blessings of the fields.
Under Persian and Greek rulers this system of irrigation requiring constant supervision was maintained, and Babylonia retained her position, though
under foreign rule. Rome, on the other hand,
strongly entrenched herself at the northern pole of

the current stretching across Asia Minor, but neglected the other pole. Byzantium as the capital of
the Eastern Roman Empire, changing its name to
Constantinople in 330 A.D., became a mighty bulwark,
ensuring Roman control of the highway up to the
Cilician gates, but in order to hold the plains and
regions beyond—the " Fertile Crescent "—the grasp
on the other pole should have been equally firm.
Her failure to do so was a fatal error. *Hinterland*
and " Fertile Crescent " stand and fall together. An
empire in the East requires firm possession of both
as the condition of permanence. The force of the
Roman power, so tenacious where its energy was at
its height, appears to have spent itself by the time it
had reached Mesopotamia.

It is significant that Pompey was unable to suppress the Parthian Empire, founded by Mithridates I
(c. 170–138 B.C.), which succeeded in wresting Babylonia from Seleucidian rulers; and though this Parthian Empire never attained to the position of the old
Persian Empire, of which it claimed to be the continuation, it retained possession of Mesopotamia
against Roman attempts to seize it, though finally
obliged in the days of Augustus to recognize a nominal Roman suzerainty. In 226 A.D. the Arsacid
rulers were forced to submit to Ardashir I, a descendant of Sasan, from whom these rulers derived their
designation as Sassanians. This new power, orig-
inating in Persia, represents a genuine revival of the
national Iranian element. It maintained itself till
the middle of the seventh century when the rise of
the Arabs put an end to it. During this period conflicts between the Sassanian rulers and the Eastern
Roman Empire took place almost incessantly. The
prize for which the Sassanians fought was northern

Mesopotamia (which had remained in Roman hands) and Asia Minor. The tide of war flowed and ebbed during the following centuries but without a decisive issue, because neither the Emperors of Byzantium nor the Sassanians, holding southern Mesopotamia, were able to control the entire stretch of the highway across Asia Minor. Finally, at the beginning of the seventh century Chosroes II penetrated as far as Chalcedon, opposite Constantinople, and by virtue of this success, was, for a short period, master of the East.

During the rule of the Parthians and Sassanians, moreover, Mesopotamia lost much of her former strength and prosperity owing to the state of neglect into which the canal system had been allowed to fall. The greater interest of the rulers lay in the region to the east of the Tigris. Although they continued to reside in Ctesiphon, on the Tigris, the chief monuments of their reigns are to be found in Persia. The Iranian character of the empire, thus emphasized, became the source of its strength, but its rise to a world power would only have been possible had the rulers recognized the region adjacent to the Persian Gulf as the prop of their empire. With only an indifferent hold on this region and allowing it to fall into decay, they could not avail themselves of their temporary success in controlling Asia Minor up to Constantinople. A few years after Chosroes II had secured Chalcedon, the counter movement began and by 627 A.D. the Eastern Emperor Heraclius had driven the Sassanians back to the Persian Gulf.

IX

The long-continued struggle between Rome and Persia for the possession of Asia Minor as the key to the East thus ended in enfeebling both empires, and making room for a force of an entirely different character that emerges from a region whence one least expected it—Arabia. Mohammed, the Apostle of Allah (c 570–632 A.D.), founds the religion of Islam, and inspiring the scattered Arab tribes also with a national ideal unites them into a solid mass. Under remarkably able generals, Arabic armies pour forth out of Arabia to win the world for the propagation of the gospel of their prophet. The region of the Persian Gulf marks their first conquest, and Constantinople at the other end their goal. Within a year of Mohammed's death, the Moslem hosts make their appearance in southern Mesopotamia and put an end to the Sassanian Empire. Palestine and Egypt fall into their hands. The necessity, however, of holding the *Hinterland* also in order to maintain an Arab Empire is recognized by their leaders. Under the banner of the prophet, Islam forces its way through Asia Minor, and in 668 A.D. Constantinople was besieged by the Arabs and again in the year 674. Had the Arabs, who now held the one pole at the Persian Gulf, succeeded in capturing and retaining Constantinople in their hands, the entire East would have remained at their mercy. The check which they received in France through Charles Martel at Tours in 732 A.D. is generally regarded as marking the definite limitation to Arabic advance. It had this result merely because the Arabs failed to keep the two poles, across which ran the highway the possession of which meant the sway over the East. The real failure of Islam was in the East. The Arabs were forced back from the gates of Constantinople, and another attempt in 718 to take Constantinople was successful for a short time only. In contrast to the Romans who held Constantinople

at the one end of the chain but could not maintain
the other, the Arabs held the region of the Persian
Gulf but not the other. For this reason the building up of a great united Arabic empire commanding
the East was impossible. Portions of Asia Minor
along the main roads were in their possession, but
never the whole of it. The Eastern Empire kept
its hand on the northwestern end.

The conquests of the Arabs carried out with such
remarkable rapidity soon split up into groups. Instead of a central authority in Mecca, rival caliphates
arose in Mesopotamia, Egypt and Spain. The
strongest of these was the one which had its seat
in Bagdad founded by the Caliph Mansur in 763 A.D.,
close by the site of Ctesiphon and not far from ancient
Babylon. A glorious day dawned once more for
this time-honored region which reached its high-
noon in the days of Harun al-Rashid (786–809 A.D.),
but again we note the fateful verdict of history that
without the control of the *Hinterland*, sharply defined
limitations are prescribed to the extension of any
Mesopotamian power. The caliphs of Bagdad could
not regain Egypt, nor could they always quell dis-
turbances in Syria. Realizing the importance of Asia
Minor in order to make their own position secure,
the Abbasid rulers of Bagdad made frequent expeditions in that direction. In the year 833 A.D., it
looked as though the ambition to hold Constantinople would be finally realized. With such success
had the caliph Mamun penetrated into the heart of
Asia Minor that the Byzantine Emperor Theophilus
sued for peace. Mamun refused the offer, and death
alone prevented him from carrying out his design to
seize the capital of the Eastern Roman Empire.
It was the last effort of the kind. In another cen-

tury a new force came to the front in Asia Minor
which, while it postponed the downfall of the Eastern Roman Empire, also blocked the Arabic advance.
Nor was it long before it gathered sufficient strength
to threaten both the Arabs and the Emperors at Constantinople.   These new aspirants for control of Asia
Minor with the ambition to secure *both* poles of the
current were the Turks.

X

Asia Minor, we have seen, was destined by her
geographical position to be at the mercy of hordes
pouring into the region from time immemorial from
Central Asia.   Wave after wave surges across the
Caucasus or by a more direct route.   It was thus
that the Hittites came, and possibly the Ægeans,
the Cimmerians and other hordes, while the Gauls
came across the Hellespont,—and now the region is
threatened by two other motley groups—the Turks
and the Mongols.   Into the ethnic problem suggested by these new invaders we need not enter.   An
ultimate connection between the two seems probable,
but as they come upon the horizon of history they
appear quite distinct, the Turks being far more capable of assimilating the culture of the region into
which they came or were driven, than the Mongols,
who appear more in the light of raiders, and after
accomplishing their purpose pass back to whence
they came.   The Turks are the first to appear.

We hear of them towards the middle of the sixth
century of our era occupying a district on the Oxus
and victorious over opponents.   In the following
century they assist the Byzantine Emperor Heraclius (610–641 A.D.) in his campaigns against the Sassanian empire.   Splitting up into smaller groups their

PRIMITIVE IRRIGATION IN MESOPOTAMIA

THE PORTAL AT NIGDEH. SELYUK ART. (C. 1223 A.D.)

trend is westward, and they gradually spread over a large region. A branch advances into Asia Minor, driven perhaps by waves behind it. This advance guard becomes known as the Seljuk Turks, though the name does not appear till the eleventh century, when we find them firmly established in Asia Minor and in control of most of it, as far east as Cappadocia and south to Cilicia. In 1071 they defeat the Byzantine Emperor, and in 1080 take Nicæa which brings them close to the Bosphorus.

The Seljuk Turks had become Moslems as had other branches of the Turks when coming into contact with Arabs and Persians. They thus added to the strength of Mohammedan control of the East. We find them spreading in all directions until by the thirteenth century there was scarcely any part of the Nearer East in which Turks were not to be found, serving as mercenaries or otherwise engaged in the service of the various caliphates. The sultans of Rum, as the dominion of the Seljuk Turks in Asia Minor came to be called, with their capital at Iconium (modern Konia) were patrons of art, and remains of Seljuk constructions in Asia Minor testify to the distinction and grace acquired by this branch of the Turkish race in architecture and decoration.

But while Turks thus commingled with the subjects of the Arabic caliphates, they never formed a union with them and contributed rather to the further splitting up of Asia Minor and the region of the " Fertile Crescent " into independent sections. The Abbasid caliphs were left in possession of their authority, though the Seljuk Sultans were the masters of the situation. They held Syria and threatened Egypt at various times. On the other hand, the

Seljuk Turks, though a constant menace to the
Byzantine Empire, lacked the background necessary
to the establishment of a strong world empire in
the East. The control of Asia Minor by the Seljuk
Turks, moreover, coincides with the age of the
Crusades, which begins in 1096 and continues till
1291, when the last of the strongholds on the Phœnician coast fell into Moslem hands. This long-
continued attempt on the part of Christian Europe
to secure possession of the Land illustrates again
the thesis suggested by the history of Asia Minor.
that without this region no grasp on the Near East
can be effective.

XI

On the surface, the Crusades were undertaken
to rescue the Holy Sepulchre and other sites sacred
to Christians out of Moslem hands, but their deeper
significance lies in the endeavor that they represent
to save the Near East for Christendom. Despite the
split between Eastern and Western Christendom,
the Western Crusaders in reality came to the aid of
the Byzantine Empire, and while the Crusades failed
ultimately in their purpose, they, like the coming
of the Turks, postponed the downfall of Constantinople for two centuries and more. It has been properly pointed out that the Crusades can only be under-
stood when considered as a part of Eastern History,[19]
more particularly of that part of the East covered by
Asia Minor and those countries for which it forms
the *Hinterland*. The Crusades represent a struggle
for possession of the East, precisely of the same
order as the various struggles which we have rapidly

---

[19] So by Stevenson in his admirable work, *The Crusaders in
the East* (Cambridge, 1907).

set forth in this survey of the salient features of the history of the highway from Constantinople to the Persian Gulf. The religious motive underlying the Crusades does not offset their real meaning when viewed from the broader standpoint of human history as largely dominated by three factors, climate, geographical position and economic pressure, or the reaction from such pressure. The recovery of holy sites is an incidental feature of the Crusades. The essential feature is the endeavor to secure the Near East as necessary for the normal development of the West in all directions—in commerce, in religious thought, in cultural stimulus, in art and even in science.

The Crusades are, therefore, a part of the " trend towards the East " which has always been a motive power in western lands and has in our own days given rise to the Bagdad Railway as its latest manifestation. The course that the Crusades take, likewise furnishes another illustration of the impossibility of holding Palestine—the goal of the religious hosts—without the *Hinterland.* Strange and yet natural that the first battles of the Crusades should be waged in Asia Minor. Nicæa falls into their hands in June, 1097, Antioch in June, 1098, and Jerusalem in July, 1099. A Latin Kingdom was established amidst great enthusiasm with Godfrey of Bouillon as King. It lasted amid great difficulties till 1187, when Jerusalem was captured by Sultan Saladin. The surprise is that it endured so long, for surrounded as the Crusaders were by enemies, no power could possibly be established in Palestine with Asia Minor still held largely by the Seljuk Turks, and the rest of it broken up into little states.

The dissensions among the Crusaders were no doubt a factor in leading to the weakness of their hold on other centres like Antioch and Edessa, which were made the capitals of little principalities, but the main reason for their failure was the lack of the *Hinterland*. They passed through Asia Minor but never held it. A Latin control was effected for a time at Constantinople from 1204 to 1261, but this victory over the Greek element in the Byzantine Empire was of little avail, with the highway that starts opposite Constantinople in control of Moslem groups, or at the mercy of the hordes that again began to pour into the region from Central Asia.

The Seljuk Turks, as well as other branches that had established themselves in Syria, Khorassan, Karman, Irak and up to Afghanistan and had made themselves independent, were all swept away by the surge of a Mongol invasion under Jenghis Khan in 1219. History repeats itself once more in the manner in which Jenghis Khan and his successors overrun Asia Minor, and then obtain possession of the lands lying beyond the Cilician gates and the Amanus range. The Bagdad caliphate falls before the attack of Hulagu Khan, the brother of Jenghis, in 1258. Syria and Palestine yield to the invader two years later and Egypt is threatened.

XII

The tide is turned through a fortunate chance which brings another branch of the Turkish race to the front. In 1227 a horde of several thousand Turks are driven from their settlements in Khorassan through the pressure of the Mongol invasion. They first seek refuge near Erzerum and afterwards pass on towards Angora, under the leadership of Ertoghrul. These are the Ottoman, or, perhaps more properly, the Osmanli Turks who become the founders of the present Turkish Empire. They take their name from Osman or Othman,[20] the son of Ertoghrul. Ertoghrul and his followers come to the aid of the Seljuk Turks and near Angora (1260 A.D.) inflict a crushing blow on Hulagu, who in view of the menace abandons the attempt to advance to Egypt and hurries back to the north. The Mongol generals left in command in Syria are defeated by Sultan Kutuz of Egypt about the same time that the forces of the Greeks and the Mongols under Hulagu are pursued to the Hellespont. The danger of the Mongolian invasion had passed, but it is again significant that it is their defeat in Asia Minor which decides the fate of the East. The victory being due to Ertoghrul, he receives as his reward the district around Eskishehr (ancient Dorylaeum) in the northwest of Asia Minor. With this as a starting-point, the power of the Ottoman Turks develops under Osman (1289–1326) and his successors, Orkhan (1326–1359), Murad I (1359–1389), and Bayezid (1389–1403), to a commanding position in the East, though not as yet dominant. They devoted their efforts towards obtaining control of the region in northwestern Asia Minor up to the Bosphorus. In 1338 they reach Haidar Pasha directly opposite Constantinople, and the starting-point of the Bagdad Railway. It should always be remembered that the foothold of the Turks in Europe was

---

[20] According to H. A. Gibbons, *The Foundation of the Ottoman Empire* (New York, 1916), p. 6, Osman is the pronunciation in Constantinople, Othman in Asia Minor.

secured through the court quarrels at Constantinople, which led John Cantacuzenus who had himself
proclaimed Emperor, to call in the aid of Orkhan
against Anna, the widow of Andronicus III, whose
counsellor Cantacuzenus had been. This was in 1341.
In a few years the Ottomans aid in capturing Adrianople, which becomes the capital of the Ottoman
Empire in 1367. Thrace falls into their hands, Mace-
donia is colonized by Moslems, and by the end of
the fourteenth century they hold a preponderant
position in the Balkan Peninsula. The Balkan question which was the immediate cause for the war of
1914 thus takes its rise over five centuries ago.

The victory of Murad at Kossovo in 1389 puts an
end to Serbian independence. Under Bayezid, raids
are made into Hungary. Constantinople is besieged
in 1391 and again in 1395, and Bayezid defeats a force
composed of the best European chivalry, co-operating
with Sigismund of Hungary, at Nicopolis in Bulgaria
in 1396. Greece is invaded in the following year.
But while the Osmanli were thus making themselves the peers of the Byzantine Empire in Europe,
they were neglecting to strengthen themselves in
Asia Minor. Content with holding a small section
of it, the remainder was split up into a large number of independent states or Emirates.[21] It is not
until the reign of Bayezid that we find an attempt
made to put an end to this condition by a vigorous
campaign which, beginning in 1392, lasted for several
years but only resulted in obtaining possession of the
northern part of Asia Minor. Whether due to the

---

[21] See Appendix B to Gibbons' work, *Foundation of the
Ottoman Empire,* who gives a full list of such states, and adds
an interesting summary of the results of his investigation of
the state of Asia Minor during the fourteenth century.

feeling of security inspired by the final defeat of the
Latin Crusaders in 1291, or to a reliance on the
Moslemization of Asia Minor as a guarantee against
dangers from this side, the policy of the Ottoman
Turks in striking for the control of Eastern Europe
instead of making themselves masters of Asia Minor
was a fatal error, which came near resulting in their
complete extinction through another Mongol invasion, as terrific in its onslaught as the previous one
under Jenghis Khan.

The leader was Timur, who after a remarkable
sweep which brought a wide stretch from western
India to Armenia and which included Persia, Mesopotamia and the steppes between the Black and
Caspian seas under subjection, between 1399 and
1402 overran Asia Minor and made Bayezid his
prisoner. By the irony of fate the decisive defeat
of Bayezid took place at Angora—the strategic
point where the Ottomans 140 years previous had
gained their first victory which started them on their
career. By the end of 1402 when Smyrna fell into
his hands, Timur had established his position as the
heir of the Ottoman Empire. He is hailed by Christian Europe as the savior of Europe from Moslem
domination, and the hope is expressed by Henry IV
of England that he may by conversion to Christian-
ity become the champion of the Cross. But Timur,
like Jenghis Khan, was after all a raider rather than
an invader. The Mongols, in contrast to the Turks,
left no indelible impress of their astonishingly rapid
conquests beyond the work of destruction in their
wake. There was no constructive element in either
of the Mongolian invasions, and having finished his
work of destruction Timur leaves Asia Minor as

suddenly as he came, and dies in 1405 while on his
way to further raids upon China.

XIII

Had Timur followed up his defeat of Bayezid
by an effort at organization, the empire of the Ottomans would have disappeared, or had the states of
Christian Europe availed themselves of the inter-
regnum (1403–1413) between the defeat of Bayezid
and the revival of Ottoman power under Mohammed I, a son of Bayezid (1413–1421), to restore the
Eastern Roman Empire—now reduced to a pitiful
extreme—the history of the world might have taken
a different turn. Instead, after the sudden departure
of Timur, the Emperor Manuel Palaeologus appeals
to Mohammed I who had established himself at
Brusa, for aid against another son of Bayezid, who
after seizing Adrianople laid siege to Constantinople. Mohammed defeats his brother Mussa in
1413, and before his death succeds in regaining all
the territory over which his father had ruled—an
amazing renaissance, indicative of the recuperative
powers of the Turks. The Turkish navy was organized in his days as an adjunct to the army. Mohammed I carries out a more energetic policy in strengthening his hold on Asia Minor. His son and successor Murad II (1421–1451)[22] continues this policy,
and it is not until he knows the *Hinterland* to be
secure that he felt free to direct in person the further
conquest of Europe. Salonica is taken in 1428, further advances are made into Servia and Hungary but
are checked by troubles that had broken out in Asia

---

[22] Murad II abdicated in 1444 in favor of his son (then
only 14 years old), but was forced by turbulent conditions to
resume his throne.

Minor.   After his son Mohammed II (1451–1481)
had finally succeeded in quelling the revolts that were
constantly breaking out, the final act in the drama
of the contest between Cross and Crescent that had
been going on for centuries was staged by the taking of Constantinople on the 20th of May, 1453. The
last Byzantine Emperor, Constantine Palaeologus,
fell among the defenders of the last bulwark.

The taking of Constantinople is one of the decisive events in history, because it symbolizes the
final triumph of the Crescent in the East. The dura-
bility of this triumph is illustrated by the futility
of all efforts during the succeeding centuries down
to our days to change the aspect of the Near East
as a Mohammedan possession, which even the energetic missionary efforts of the various bodies of the
Christian church, praiseworthy and useful as they
have been in promoting education, have been unable
to affect to any material extent. The reason for
this is once more to be sought in the possession
of the highway stretching across Asia Minor which,
after the definite control of the one end by the Ottomans, was gradually made equally firm at the other
end—at the Persian Gulf. Before Mohammed II
passed away, Asia Minor had been completely sub-
jugated, and under his successor, Selim I (1512–
1520), Persia, Hindustan, Egypt, Syria and the coast-
line of Arabia became part of the Turkish Empire.
The control of the *Hinterland* made the Ottoman
Sultans masters of the East—precisely as this control had been a decisive factor ever since the days
of antiquity. The rise of the Ottoman Turks to the
rank of a world-power having been thus brought
about by the firm grasp of the historic highway, its
permanency was conditioned upon maintaining its

hold. Once more we note that the key to the Eastern situation lies not in the Balkan Peninsula nor
in the possession of Constantinople, but in the strategic character of the route connecting Constantinople with Bagdad—as illustrated by the constant
repetition of events, though under changed outward
circumstances from the times of Mursil, the Hittite,
in the middle of the thirteenth century before this
era to Mohammed II, the Osmanli Turk in the middle of the fifteenth century of our era—an astonishing
example of historical continuity for over 2700 years, as
a result of the geographical position of Asia Minor.

The taking of Constantinople, marking the control of the highway of which it forms the starting-
point, meant the raising of an impassable barrier
to the East, erected against any further efforts of
Christian and Western Europe to break through it.
The year 1453 marks the real end of the Crusades,
viewed in their broader historical significance as the
endeavor to save the access to the East for Europe.
A direct consequence of the capture of Constantinople was the stimulus given to navigation to find a
new route to the East by sea. Columbus sailed west
in the hope of making good by a water route to India
what had been lost through the failure of the Crusades
to keep the land highway to the East open to western
nations. A new continent is discovered by accident
in the search for this route in 1492, and the Cape
of Good Hope is rounded by Vasco da Gama in
1477 in the endeavor to find a more direct sea
route to the East. The " trend towards the East,"
manifesting itself in such a variety of forms, appears
to be an ineradicable longing that the West received
when it fell heir to the high culture that arose in

the ancient East. The "call of the East" still resounds in the ears of contemporary Europe, and America. It is the impelling force behind commercial exploitation and the construction of railways to the East. So closely intertwined is the fate of the West upon access to the East that the taking of Constantinople leads to the discovery of America. One is inclined to put it strongly that after the closing up of the highway across Asia Minor, there was nothing for Columbus to do but to discover America—and he did it.

XIV

The Ottoman rulers, however, failed to recognize that their position in the world depended upon their being and remaining an eastern power. In their endeavors to become also a western power, they sinned, as it were, against their own destiny and brought about the downfall of a great empire. They tried like Janus to face in both directions, instead of keeping their gaze steadily turned toward the East. Actuated by ambitions to overstep natural barriers to their extension, they became, as has always been the inevitable fate of attempts at world power, a menace to the world.

The height of the Turkish Empire was reached in the reign of Suleiman I (1520–1566), whose surname "the Magnificent" symbolizes the climax attained. Belgrade was captured in 1521, Budapest in 1528. The gates of Vienna are reached in 1529, and Suleiman prepared for a contest at arms with the Emperor Charles V. The Moslemization of Europe seemed imminent, and when Suleiman died in 1566, the Turkish Empire extended close to the frontiers of Germany.

The decline may be dated from the battle of

Lepanto in October, 1571, when Don John of Austria destroyed the menace of the Turkish fleet, which had secured control of the African coast to Morocco and had endangered Italy, Spain and France.   Worn out by almost continuous wars in Europe and the suppression of revolts in Asia Minor and Persia for a stretch of over thirty years, the Turks concluded a peace at Sitvatorok (in Hungary) in November, 1606, which put an end to their period of conquest. From now on, the efforts of the Ottoman Sultans are directed towards maintaining their dominions with a steady decline of their power in Europe, though it was not until well towards the close of the eighteenth century that the defensive power of the Empire was broken to the extent of forcing upon her onerous terms of peace.   The treaty of Kutchuk Kainarji (in Bulgaria) signed in July, 1774, between Russia and Turkey marks another turning-point which definitely gave to Russia the ascendancy.   In 1792 the Crimea was added to Russia by the treaty of Jassy.   The next century saw the struggle of Turkey to retain possession of the states of the Balkan Peninsula, with the gradual loss of one after the other until her European possessions were reduced to the comparatively small corner at the southeastern extremity, which now represents all that is left of what was once a formidable dominion.

But Turkey was still an Eastern power after having been shorn of her European possessions.   Despite uprisings and revolts in Persia and Syria and Egypt, she had managed to retain her control of the Nearer East by holding the highway across Asia Minor.   During the seventeenth century, however, her hold on the one end at the Persian Gulf was loosened.   She was forced to make a supreme effort to put down independent movements that were taking place in Mesopotamia to throw off the yoke. Since the days of Suleiman more particularly, the Mesopotamian plain had been neglected. The canal systems were not kept in repair, and Bagdad itself lost its prestige and its magnificence. The country went backward steadily. Turkish misrule completed the havoc wrought by the submerging of large districts through the annual overflow of the two rivers, now no longer directed into the fields. Though still strong at one end of the chain, the links at the other end grew weaker and affected the resistance power of the chain as a whole. A situation arose as in the days of the Roman occupancy, which similarly began to fail with the loosening of the grip at the Persian Gulf.

XV

The possibility of a decided break in the current stretching from Constantinople and Bagdad was foreshadowed by Napoleon's expedition to Egypt in 1798, which came as a complete surprise to Turkey herself. With the keen insight of a military genius, Napoleon, dreaming of the exploits of world conquerors of the past—Cyrus, Alexander and their successors to Mohammed II—saw that the East was to be conquered and Turkey eliminated not by way of Europe, but through the East. His occupation of Egypt was merely the preliminary step. His design as shown by his siege of Acre on the Palestinian coast was to make himself master of Syria, and thence to threaten the possession of the Asia Minor Highway—to cut the chain as it were at a strategic point. Egypt was merely a passage-way to Palestine which, as we have seen, had always played the part of a bulwark for Egypt against attacks from

Asia Minor. Napoleon was hastily called back to Egypt, and after the battle of Abukir returned to France where disturbing conditions had arisen during his absence. He was thus forced to abandon further designs. It is, of course, somewhat precarious in default of definite evidence to speculate as to what was in his mind, but the expedition to Syria is significant as an index of his plans. In the case of a military genius it is not essential to assume that he forms his plans through a conscious knowledge of past history, though Napoleon was a student of the past. Insight often anticipates the conclusions of the investigator. As an expert in strategy, he would have had no difficulty in recognizing that a successful attack on the highway leading from Constantinople to Bagdad would have spelled the end of Ottoman domination of the East.

However this may be, the expedition to Egypt marks the beginning of the attempt on the part of Europe to recover the direct access to the East. It is the first turn in the unwinding of the chain of those events which in the past had led to the triumph of the Crescent over the Cross. The barrier set up by the grasp of the route from Constantinople to Bagdad in the hands of a Moslem power was to be thrown down, and the route to be restored to Christian Europe. This European struggle for the control of the East which thus begins with Napoleon is in a manner a new crusade, though the meaning of the symbols have changed, and the Cross stands for the restless spirit of progress marked by commercial and political expansion, and the Crescent for the fatalistic conservatism of an incrustated civilization. As in the Middle Ages, all the great European Powers are participating in this new crusade—France, Eng-

land, Russia, Austria, Italy, and as the last comer
the resuscitated Germany, reunited into a mighty
empire in 1871.

The history of Europe since the end of the eighteenth century is largely taken up with the ambitions
of the Powers to secure a slice of the Near East,
though before the process of dissolution in the Near
East sets in we find the historic highway once more
playing a decisive rôle.   In 1833 the Ottoman Empire
virtually lost its control of Egypt through the treaty
of Kutaia (Asia Minor) with Mehemet Ali, which
not only recognized the latter's authority as heredi-
tary Pasha of Egypt, but made him also master of
Syria up to the Cilician gates.   The treaty followed
upon the successful campaign which Ibrahim Pasha,
the son of Mehemet Ali, waged in 1831–1832 against
the Sultan Mahmud II.   Ibrahim Pasha led the
Egyptian troops victoriously through the historic
highway to Konia—once the residence of the Seljuk
Sultans—where he inflicted a crushing defeat on
the Turkish army and captured its commander,
Reshid Pasha. At the Cilician gates, as the strategic
point, he erected fortifications which are still to be
seen.   The control of this highway was thus lost for
the Turkish Empire, and the loss would have been
absolute but for the intervention of Russia.   In 1839
the Sultan made an attempt to regain his prestige in
Asia Minor, but Ibrahim was victorious at Nisibin
near Birejik on the Euphrates.[23]   The Ottoman
Empire was once more in a critical position, from

---

[23] It is interesting to note that the famous Moltke was
present at this battle as adviser to Hafiz Pasha, and wrote an
account of it in his "Letters from Turkey," which he published in 1841 ("Briefe Aus der Türkei) of which a French
translation appeared in 1872 and an Italian one in 1877.

which this time it was saved by the European Powers whose intervention now became more active—and intervention meant partition.

England established her protectorate over Egypt, France definitely took Algiers, Russia made her peace with England to share in the domination over Persia, Austria acquired a sphere of influence over Palestine and snatched Bosnia and Herzogovina as stepping-stones leading to the great highway. Italy has seized Tripoli, and France obtained a dominant position over Syria through railway concessions, while England with keen foresight secured navigation control at the Persian Gulf to Bagdad. Lastly, Germany by a master stroke obtained the concession of a railway across the historic highway from Constantinople to Bagdad—with the privilege of extension to the Persian Gulf, and with important branch roads at various points of commercial and strategic importance. The control of this highway by any European power—whether Germany, England or France—must lead to the end of Ottoman domination of the Near East. It would mark in every sense of the word the close of an era and the opening of a new one, that would have its effect on the entire world. The force of the change would sweep away all endeavors of any modern power, engaged in world commerce, to remain in a state of political isolation. The fate of the Near East once more lies in the hands of Western nations. Its future will be determined by the disposition that will be made of the highway across Asia Minor.

XVI

The course of events in the Near East since the entering wedge represented by Napoleon's expedition to Egypt is thus to be interpreted as the irresistible onslaught of the West to break down the barrier created in 1453. As we survey the successive steps in this onslaught, the struggle between France and England culminating in the convention of 1904, which gave France a dominant position in Morocco in return for allowing England a free hand in Egypt, the attempts of France and Russia to hedge in England in India,[24] followed by England and Russia, in dividing up their " spheres of influence " in Persia, the commercial and railway concessions secured by England, France and Russia from Turkey, sinking ever deeper into a slough of desperate weakness, we see how these struggles, conventions and partnerships all lead up to the dramatic climax—the struggle for the historic highway which is the key to the Nearer East. Its possession will mean in the future as it always has in the past—domination over Syria, Mesopotamia, Egypt and probably Arabia; and the Near East points its finger directly towards the Farther East. Under the modern symbol of railway control, Asia Minor, true to the genius of its history, once more looms up as a momentous factor in the world history. The war of 1914 has brought the events of the past to another turning-point in the political kaleidoscope. The story of the Bagdad Railway is thus crucial for an understanding of the crisis that was a large factor in bringing on the great war, even though at the time it appeared to be a hidden feature because of the accidental occurrence that brought the European crisis to an issue. The murder at Sarajevo was merely the match applied to the pile all ready to be kindled.

---

[24] See below, p. 89.

6

CHAPTER III

THE STORY OF THE BAGDAD RAILWAY

I

THE Bagdad Railway project, or, to give its official title, " La Société Impériale Ottomane du Chemin de Fer de Bagdad," was definitely launched in 1903 by a diplomatic agreement (known as a convention), dated March 5th, between the Turkish government and a syndicate of Germans, organized as the Société du Chemin de Fer Ottoman d' Anatolie (Anatolian Railway Company). This company had obtained, in 1888, from the Turkish government the concession to build a railway, stretching from Haidar Pasha (opposite Constantinople) to Angora that has played such a notable part in Asia Minor history—a distance of 576 kilometres, or about 360 miles,[1] under a guarantee from the Turkish government of an annuity of 15,000 francs per kilometre. British capital was originally represented in the company, but was subsequently bought out by the German Syndicate so that the Anatolian company became a purely

---

[1] To be quite accurate, a short section from Haidar Pasha to Ismid on the sea of Marmora—91 kilometres—had been constructed in 1871–73 under the superintendence of Dr. Wilhelm von Pressel (see below, p. 86, note), by the Turkish government. The road was built to give the Sultan Abdul Aziz readier access to his shooting-box at Ismid. This section was taken over by the Anatolian Railway Company at the time that the concession was given to extend it to Angora.

VIEW OF ANGORA, ON THE ANATOLIAN RAILWAY

VIEW OF KONIA ON THE BAGDAD RAILWAY

German enterprise.   The railway was begun in 1889
and completed in 1893.   A further concession to extend the road to Konia from the junction Eskishehr
(the ancient Dorylæum) on the Angora line—a distance of 444 kilometres or about 280 miles—was obtained in 1893 under an annuity guarantee of 13,892
francs per kilometre.[2] This branch was completed in
1896. A concession accorded at the same time to
continue the Angora line to Cæsarea and eventually
to Diarbekr and Bagdad was abandoned by the company, in favor of a much more ambitious plan which
was brought forward as a result of the visit of the
German Emperor to the Sultan Abdul Hamid in
1898. A German commission was empowered to survey a line cutting transversely across Asia Minor from
Konia, following largely the historic highway along
which the armies of so many peoples and lands had
passed forward and backward for thousands of years,
emerging from the Taurus range into the plain
through the famous Cilician gates, thence across the
Amanus range eastwards to Mosul and south to
Bagdad.[3] A German cruiser, the Ancora, was at
the same time sent to examine the conditions at the
proposed terminus of the line on the Persian Gulf.
Angora, Konia, the Cilician gates, Adana, Mosul,

---

[2] The reduction was perhaps due to the estimated lower
cost of the very simple construction of the branch on an
easy level.

[3] It is said that the Sultan, realizing the importance of
the railway in the event of war, was particularly insistent
that the main road was to avoid any approach to the coast
so as to avert the danger of a bombardment through a hostile
fleet. The transverse route across the historic highway fulfils
this condition.

Bagdad would link this enterprise in a most romantic fashion with the most famous landmarks in the history of Asia Minor and of Mesopotamia, which, we have seen, cannot be separated from Asia Minor in any historical or geographical survey of the region. The fate of the one determines the fate of the other. On November 27th, 1899, Dr. Siemens, the Director of the Deutsche Bank and President of the Anatolian Railway Company, announced the scheme, though for the present only the general policy of the concession had been agreed upon by the Turkish government. Over two years were to elapse before on January 16th, 1902, an Irade of the Sultan approved the convention, which was naturally hailed with great enthusiasm in Germany. The Anatolian Railway Company, however, found the undertaking too difficult to handle under its management alone, and accordingly a supplementary company—the above-named Société du Chemin de Fer de Bagdad—was organized to carry out the larger scheme in co-operation with the Anatolian company. A new convention was therefore drawn up in March, 1903, in which the Bagdad Railway Company appears as the successor to the Anatolian Company, though the parties interested in both were the same. By this convention, the concession was extended to Basra, a stretch of about 576 kilometres, or 360 miles, below Bagdad, and it also included a number of branch lines, the three most important [4] of which were (1) one at

---

[4] The other branches contemplated and included in the convention were: (1) Toprak-Kale (near Adana) to Alexandretta, (2) from Haran (on the way to Mosul) to Urfa—the ancient Edessa, (3) Bagche to Marash, (4) to Aintab from a point near Killis. According to Woods in the Geo-

Sadijeh on the Tigris (above Bagdad) running to Hanikin, and pointing towards a union with projected railways in Persia, centering in Teheran; (2) Muslimiya to Aleppo, connecting with the Syrian and the Hedjaz railroads running to Damascus, Medina and Mecca, and (3) a branch from Zubeir (on the way to Basra) to some point on the Persian Gulf to be determined in the future.[5] The extension from Konia to Basra involved an extension of about 2264 kilometres, or about 1415 miles, making a total of about 3000 kilometres, or 1875 miles, from Haidar Pasha to Basra. Including the branches, estimated at about 800 kilometres, or 500 miles, the project would thus place in German hands the control of over 3800 kilometres, or 2375 miles,[5a] with junctions con-

---

graphical Journal for July, 1917, pages 46–47, it is possible, also that the Turkish government may have constructed since the beginning of the war, a branch from Ras el-Ain to Diarbekr, but this is not certain and has, therefore, not been included in the map. The Toprak-Kale branch was bombarded by the English in the early part of the war.

The railway distance from Bagdad to Basra can only be approximately indicated, since this section is not actually constructed. The direct distance from Bagdad to Basra is only 500 kilometres, or about 312 miles, but the route along the Tigris, with its bends and curves, increases this distance to about 800 kilometres, or 500 miles. According to the estimate of Sir William Willcocks, the railway route will cover about 360 miles.

[5] Kuweit was in the mind of the projectors, but had to be abandoned. See below p. 101.

[5a] Included in this calculation is the stretch Eskishehr-Angora of 311 kilometres, or about 194 miles, as a branch of the Bagdad Railway.

necting with the other railways of Asia Minor, Syria, Palestine, Arabia and eventually Persia—truly a magnificent enterprise that must command our admiration, the emanation of fertile brains endowed with a vision of the future.

II

The road was to be built in twelve sections of 200 kilometres each, though this item in the convention was subsequently modified. The original plan had been, as above indicated, to reach the Persian Gulf by an extension of the Angora line across Cæsarea and Diarbekr and thence along the Tigris, passing Mosul, to Bagdad and the Persian Gulf. This was the route mapped out by Dr. Wilhelm von Pressel, a distinguished German engineer [6] who had constructed the Baron de Hirsch group of railways in European Turkey and who built the first stretch of the Bagdad Railway Haidar-Pasha-Ismid for the Sultan in 1871–1873, as well as the extension to Angora and Konia. The change in favor of a transverse route from Konia marks an important turning-point in the political aspect of the enterprise. The northern route would not have interfered with English or French plans for railway extension in Asia Minor and Syria. England and France, indeed, had the right of priority in the field. As early as 1856 (September 23rd) the construction of a railway from Smyrna to Aidin had been granted to an English company which was completed in 1866 and eventually

---

[6] He died at Constantinople in 1902. Shortly before his death he published a monograph, Les Chemins de Fer en Turquie d'Asie (Zurich, 1902).

extended to Ergerdir, a distance of 470 kilometres, or about 294 miles, with four small branches totaling a little over 120 kilometres, or about 76 miles—a total, therefore, of 592 kilometres, or 370 miles. This, the oldest railway in Asia Minor, built without any guarantee from the Turkish government, is the only one that was still in English hands at the outbreak of the war. A request made in 1891 for the extension of this line to Konia was not granted. Not long afterwards, however, in 1893, the Turkish government granted the concession to extend a second line from Smyrna to Kassaba (93 kilometres, or about 58 miles), likewise organized by an English company and completed in 1897 to Afiun-Karahissar, a total distance from Smyrna of 420 kilometres, or 262 miles.[7] The Turkish government availed itself of its privilege to purchase the line in 1893 and turned it over to French capitalists. Probably the plan to extend this second line from Smyrna to a junction with a Bagdad railway, starting from Konia, was the real reason for not according the request of the English company for a prolongation to Konia. There would in that case have been two such lines from Smyrna, connecting with the Bagdad Railway. A third smaller coast line Mersina to Adana, of 67 kilometres, or about 42 miles, was originally in the hands of an Anglo-French Company, but was subsequently transferred to the Turkish government and later acquired by the Bagdad Railway Company. It was opened in 1886.

---

[7] To be accurate, a preliminary extension of 75 kilometres or 47 miles from Kassaba to Alashehr had been granted in 1872. Afiun-Karahissar is the junction with the Konia-Bagdad route. Adding a number of small branches the Smyrna-Kassaba Company operates in all 322 miles. The company was organized as far back as 1863.

III

Had the original plan of the German group to run the Bagdad Railway across northern Asia Minor from Angora been adhered to, the interior would have been kept free, and it is likely that a favorite English plan (afterwards taken up also by the French government), to run a railway from the Gulf of Alexandretta via Aleppo and the Euphrates to Bagdad might have been carried out. Far back in the middle of the nineteenth century this project had been brought forward by far-sighted British men of affairs. Sir Wm. Andrew, a railway official of wide experience in India, was particularly prominent in advocating this scheme of an Euphrates Valley Railroad, which he regarded as of the utmost importance for strengthening England's hold on India.[8] In 1857 an official report was presented to the English government by Sir John Macneill and General Chesney of the proposed route from Alexandretta as the starting-point—a much shorter and far simpler way than across the difficult Taurus range. In 1872 Sir Wm. Andrew succeeded in having a Committee of the House of Commons appointed to carefully examine into the project. The Committee reported favorably, the Turkish government was well disposed, but nothing came at the time of the splendid scheme. The Suez Canal began to absorb the public interest in England. England's ultimate possession of it and

---

[8] So according to Fraser, *Short Cut to India,* p. 32, who regards Andrew as the father of the Euphrates Railway project. In 1857 Sir Wm. Andrew published a *Memoir on the Euphrates Valley and the Route to India* (London, W. H. Allen & Co.) and again, as late as 1882, *Euphrates Valley Route to India.*

her occupation of Egypt prompted her to rest content with a shortened water route to India, as a sufficient protection for her Eastern possessions.

Had the northern route to Bagdad been followed by the German syndicate and left a southern route free for a second line in the hands of England or France, the railway projects of Asia Minor and Syria might have remained purely commercial undertakings of great cultural value, marking the economic progress of contact between East and West. The political aspect of railway plans in the Near East might have been permanently kept in the background. The European situation would have assumed an entirely different coloring, if England and Germany had not clashed in the East over the Bagdad Railway, as happened immediately upon the announcement of the convention of 1902–1903.

The stumbling block that prevented the execution of the original plan was—strangely enough—Russia. Her opposition to the northern route brought about the change. Russia had plans of her own in Asia Minor and in the lands to the East beyond. In the last two decades of the nineteenth century, Russia fearing the extension of English power in the Far East cast her eyes about for securing zones of influence that might bring her into touch with the Persian Gulf and the Indian Ocean. She secured the co-operation of France in 1891, and it is both interesting and instructive to note that the Franco-Russian alliance was originally directed against England rather than against Germany.[9]   France was to form a barrier to English expansion in India east-

[9] See Bodley's article on France in the new edition of the Encyclopædia Britannica, vol. x, p. 901.

wards by her control of Indo-China, while Russia
was to check an advance westwards by obtaining
control of Afghanistan and Beluchistan. With this
in view her interest lay in securing a hold in northern
and eastern Asia Minor, with a free hand on the
southern coast of the Black Sea. She exacted from
Turkey the Black Sea Basin agreement, formally
sanctioned in 1900, which reserved to her the right
to construct railroads in northern Asia Minor. She
never availed herself of this right, and indeed, while
busy in building military commercial roads, appeared
to oppose railway construction in Asia Minor,[10] and
finally transferred her concession in Asia Minor to
French capitalists. She wanted, however, to keep
the route clear for herself from Trebizond southwards to Diarbekr where the Mesopotamian plain
begins, and eastwards through Armenia and Persia.
In the background was also the fear that a railway,
dominating northern Asia Minor, which in case of a
war would be seized by the Turkish government
for military transportation, might threaten Russia's
zones of influence in the East. At all events, her
opposition was strong enough to secure a modification of the plan of the Bagdad railway in favor of
the transverse route which, as it turned out, gave
Germany a tremendous advantage over all rivals,
though it also brought on the opposition of England.
This opposition at the time was presumably not
unwelcome to Russia. Although at the turn from
the nineteenth century to the twentieth century the

---

[10] See Géraud in the *Nineteenth Century*, 1914, pp. 965–
969 and 1324, who dwells on this point of Russia's opposition
to railways in the Near East till 1910, when a change in her
policy ensued.

relations between Russia and Germany had become strained, through the substitution of Italy in 1882 for Russia as the third member in the Alliance with Germany and Austria, and though as a consequence the alliance with France had been diverted from its original purport to a compact against German aggression, Russia was not prepared to allow any further advantage to be gained in the East by England. On the whole she still preferred Germany, and was at any rate willing to see Germany and England fight the issue out among themselves. The "Entente Cordiale" between England and France, too, had not yet begun, though the new era was approaching which changed the entire aspect of the alignment among European powers. It eventually led England and Russia through their common fear of Germany to settle their past accounts and pool their issues in the East by an amicable division of spheres of influence in Persia in 1911, with little regard to the rights of that small nation, struggling at the time to secure a popular parliamentary form of government.[11] With the European Powers thus concerned, each with its own interests, and disseminating an atmosphere of mutual suspicion and distrust, what could the ultimate outcome be except the "European Anarchy," as Lowes Dickinson aptly calls the situation that had developed in 1914.

---

[11] See Shuster's work, *Strangling of Persia* (New York, 1912). It will be recalled that the treatment accorded to Persia by Russia and acquiesced in by the English government, aroused great indignation at the time in Great Britain.

IV

England's influence at Constantinople, paramount till 1880, had weakened since then, largely through Gladstone's opposition to the régime of Turkey, for which there was ample justification. The Armenian massacres of 1894, had shocked Europe, and Gladstone was irreconcilable in his denunciation of the "unspeakable Turk," as the Sultan and all Turkey came to be called. This, naturally, was not pleasing to Constantinople, at the time under the complete domination of Abdul Hamid. Germany was quick to seize upon the situation and under the leadership of her ambitious, restless and romantically inclined young Emperor, with his mind full of far-reaching schemes, obtained by a series of cleverly designed steps the position at the Turkish capital which England had once held. The convention of 1902–03 made it evident that Germany had stolen a march on England, and that France's prestige at Constantinople had likewise suffered through the distinct advantage that Germany would have over her in the future exploitation of Asia Minor.

The terms on which the German Syndicate obtained the concessions of the Bagdad Railway were indeed most favorable. The concession was to last for 99 years, and this included the two branches already built, Haidar-Pasha-Angora and Eskishehr-Konia. It had been assumed that the concession would not go beyond a line to Bagdad, and England felt that as long as the Persian Gulf was not to be reached, the situation would not be serious for her, either from the commercial or the political point of view. The India trade would not be diverted to the Persian Gulf in favor of the short land route, because of the double loading involved and the water trip from the Gulf to Bagdad. When, however, the precise terms of the convention became known, it was seen that the extension not only included Basra, but also contemplated a branch from Zubeir (not far from Basra) to a terminus on the Persian Gulf " to be determined," together with the right of navigation on the Shatt el-Arab and the Tigris—an exclusively English privilege—during the period of construction of the Railway in this region. That gave an entirely new interpretation to the convention as a whole and at once created a critical situation which steadily grew worse.

The new Bagdad Railway Company was to be capitalized at 15 million francs, of which only one-half was to be paid up. As in the case of the Anatolian Railway there was to be a guarantee on the part of the Turkish government, fixed at an annuity of 11,000 francs per kilometre, with an additional guarantee of 4500 francs per kilometre per year for the management of the railway. The receipts above this, up to 10,000 francs per kilometre per year, to go to the Turkish government and above this amount, 60 per cent. to the government and 40 per cent. to the company. The sum needed for each section, fixed at 54 million francs, was to be placed at the disposal of the company through loans to be issued by the government, and the interest on the loan was further assured out of the coffers of the *Dette Publique*.[12] With such a guarantee, the invest-

---

[12] On this Turkish institution, setting aside fixed revenues of the Turkish Empire from definite sources under the control of the European creditors of Turkey and for their protection, see the article on Turkey in the Encyclopædia Britannica, pp. 437, 438.

ment of the German syndicate was a safe one, with scarcely any risks and under assurances of a good return. Moreover, since the material for the road would naturally be supplied from Germany— and free of duty—the profits of construction would all accrue to German firms. From this point of view alone the project meant a great boon to the German industries.

The " kilometre guarantee " worked so well in the case of the first section of the road from Konia to Bulgurli, that by dint of economy the construction actually cost about 25 million francs less than the amount secured through the loan.[13] There was thus left a handsome surplus for the syndicate, though one that was in danger, to be sure, of being wiped out by the far greater cost involved in the second section across mountain passes involving most difficult engineering feats. Moreover, the Bagdad Railway Company sold the annual guarantee of 4500 francs per kilometre for the running of the road to the Anatolian Company (*i.e.,* the German syndicate sold to itself) for 3200 francs. The difference gave the Bagdad Company an annual income of 160,000 francs, with which it could do what it pleased. Apparently the lower sum was all that the investment called for, and the rest was a " bonus " for the investors. Plenty of time was given both for beginning the work on each section after it had been decided upon—18 months—and for the completion of each section after the work had been begun, eight years. All material imported for the construction of the road was to be free from duty,

---

[13] The loan was floated in Berlin at 86.40, and thus realized somewhat over 46½ million francs.

the company was to have a monopoly of kilns erected on the route for the construction of the road, to have access to all ports and to navigation on the Euphrates and Tigris and the Shatt-el-Arab (junction with Euphrates) during the operations, and the privilege of reserving to itself the right to construct and exploit ports at Bagdad, Basra and on the Persian Gulf. In return, the Turkish government was satisfied with the demand that the workmen to be employed were to be Turkish subjects and the trains manned by Turkish officials, with the exception of the highest posts which were to be held by Germans—and that everybody connected with the railway was to wear a fez! For the present the railway was to be a single track, but the Turkish government would have the right as soon as the receipts reached an average of 30,000 francs per kilometre per year to demand the laying of a second track at the expense of the company. That contingency was remote. Years would elapse before the number of passengers and the freight could possibly defray the cost of the management of the road. Its main value would be in stimulating trade and in encouraging movements of population to the interior of Asia Minor, apart from the advantage to German industries in supplying the material for the construction— the latter a very large item indeed.

The favor shown the German syndicate was evident on the surface. Such terms had never been secured before. No wonder that there were great rejoicings in Germany when they were announced and gnashing of teeth outside of Germany.

The German syndicate, to be sure, offered to English and French capitalists a share in the enterprise. Dr. Siemens and Dr. von Gwinner, the two

leading spirits of the project, emphasized strongly
the desire to give to the undertaking an international
character,[14] but this move was generally regarded
as due to an anxiety on the part of the German
syndicate to obtain foreign capital to aid them.   It
was estimated that the cost of the Konia-Bagdad
construction would mount to 350 million francs, and
this was more than Germany was supposed to be
able to carry alone.   The control of affairs was so
arranged, it was claimed, that it would always remain in German hands.   Five of the eleven directors
were to be chosen practically by the Anatolian Company, and Germany would also be in a position to control the vote of three Ottoman representatives provided
for as members of the board, so that the Germans would
always be certain of a majority over representatives
of other shareholders.   A storm of protest against
the entire project arose in England and France, and
the two governments were severely blamed in the
press and in the legislative bodies for having permitted the convention to go through, the political
significance of which when the terms of the convention became known entirely overshadowed the
commercial aspects.   England more particularly
felt that not only were her interests in the Near
East threatened through the trade and freight that
would pass to the route of the railway, but that her
domination in India was endangered.   She had good
grounds for this fear, seeing the open manner in
which advocates of national expansion in Germany
pointed out the possibilities involved in securing

[14] Dr. von Gwinner wrote an article on the subject for
the *Nineteenth Century* (June, 1909) "*The Bagdad Railway
and the Question of British Coöperation,*" in which he declared
the Company to be open to all.

for Germany a continuous route from Hamburg to the Persian Gulf in seven or eight days, with only four additional days' journey by steamer to reach India. The Pan-Germanists, whose voice had become blatant in Germany by this time, added coals to the fire by their equally open jubilation at the prospects of a complete German control of Turkish possessions in Asia. German colonization in Asia Minor was to be encouraged, following in the wake of the commercial advantages to be gained by the railway, and thus the diplomatic supremacy of Germany in Constantinople was to be strengthened by the spread of German settlements throughout the East.

It was felt in England that if, as Napoleon is said to have remarked, Antwerp in the hands of a great continental power was a pistol leveled at the English coast, Bagdad and the Persian Gulf in the hands of Germany (or any other strong power) would be a 42-centimetre gun pointed at India.

For England, the situation that would be created at the eastern terminus of the railway—once the project was completed—would indeed be most serious; and quite apart from the political aspects of the enterprise and the danger to her far Eastern possessions, the privileges which she had enjoyed for many years through her control of navigation from the head of the Persian Gulf along the Shatt el-Arab and the Tigris would have vanished into thin air. It was from this end, therefore, that the English government attacked the problem raised by the new project.

V

England's relations with the Persian Gulf date from the time of Napoleon's expedition to Egypt in

7

1798. If the French military genius foresaw, as there is good reason to believe, that the campaign for the control of the Near East must be begun by cutting the current stretching from Constantinople to Bagdad, English statesmen foresaw with no less perspicuity that to nip the project of a control of the highway across Asia Minor in the bud, the pole at the one end needed to be secured. England, realizing at this early period the strategic importance of the Persian Gulf for safeguarding her possessions in India, proceeded to entrench herself in that region. The East India Company in the very same year that Napoleon brought his army to Egypt appointed a Resident at Bagdad to watch English interests.[15] This appointment was soon after recognized by the Turkish government, and in consequence of the risks to which the Resident was exposed, especially during a period of hostility between Turkey and England, a guard was given to him. In 1834, the post of Resident was placed under the authority of the Government of India, and the Resident was vested with consular powers. England was thus the first in the field, and indeed it was not until 1880 that other European powers began to appoint consular agents at Bagdad.

In the same year that the English Resident became an official of the government of India, navigation rights on the Euphrates were granted the firm of Lynch Brothers—three Englishmen who had settled in Bagdad as traders. In 1860 their right of steam navigation on the Shatt el-Arab, the watercourse connecting Bagdad with Basra (including the Tigris), was confirmed by the Turkish government, and they enjoy the monopoly to this day.

---

[15] " To report on French intrigue in that country," is the way Fraser, *Short Cut to India*, p. 235, puts it.

Looking to the future development of the region which in ancient times had been noted for its wealth and fertility, the English government had undertaken a careful survey of Mesopotamia extending over the years 1835–1837 under the direction of Colonel Chesney. This survey no doubt led Chesney subsequently to his advocacy of the Euphrates Valley project in order to connect the Mediterranean and the Persian Gulf by a railway as an effectual means of opening up this entire region to Western Europe, as well as furnishing the much-needed shorter route to India.

England had thus obtained a firm grasp of one end of the great highway and was determined to hold to it. Shortly after it became known that Turkey had agreed to the policy of granting an extension of the Konia line across Asia Minor, the English government took the further step of establishing a protectorate over Kuweit lying on the Persian Gulf and which, it was known, would be picked out by the Bagdad Railway Company as the eventual terminus of the stretch from Bagdad to the shore. For a long time Turkey's suzerainty over the region south of Bagdad had been purely nominal, and she was obliged to recognize the independence of several little Sultanates and Emirates in this section, among others that of Kuweit, which gave her considerable trouble. England took advantage of the situation and, championing the cause of a certain Moubarek, forced the recognition of his claims and of his independence. In return for this protection, the district around Kuweit came practically under English control. She thus put an effectual spoke into the wheel of the German syndicate several months before the convention of January, 1902, with the Anatolian Railway

Company was actually signed, and no doubt in anticipation of this contingency. It necessitated a change in the terminus to Fao (60 miles south of Basra), not as advantageous as Kuweit, and involving costly " barrage " undertakings to be carried out. Moreover, with Kuweit further south under British control, a British fleet could in case of an emergency command Fao.

British policy was determined that the railway should not reach the Persian Gulf under German control. This was clearly enunciated by Lord Cranbourne, Under-Secretary for Foreign Affairs, in January, 1902, who stated that the " maintenance of the *status quo* in the Persian Gulf was incompatible with the occupation by any Power of a port on those waters." [16] The Bagdad Railway, if extended even to Basra, would destroy the trade that English merchants and English capital had painfully built up in the most important centre between India and the Suez Canal. With Germany pushing English commerce at every point through the remarkable energy, perseverance and enterprise shown by German merchants, the English prospects for retaining the commercial supremacy in the East were not bright, but over and above this was ever the political danger involved in seeing Germany standing behind the railway project, entrenched at a port on the Persian Gulf—with nothing intervening between that sheet of water and the ports of India. The Bagdad Railway was indeed a short cut to India—but a short cut from Berlin, not from London. The Suez Canal which was the English " short cut " would be brought

[16] Quoted by Géraud in the *Nineteenth Century*, 1914, (June) p. 1317.

into rivalry with the Asia Minor route which was the shorter cut, to the disadvantage of the former in almost every respect.

VI

The delay between the announcement of the concession of the Konia-Bagdad route in November, 1899, and the drawing up of the convention in January, 1902, was due in part to the protests voiced in England, France and Russia, in part to negotiations with the Turkish government in regard to details, and in part to preparations needed for so gigantic an undertaking. The German Emperor visited England in November, 1899, and obtained, so it is said, the promise of a free hand in Asia Minor from Mr. Chamberlain, but fresh difficulties must have arisen when the full significance of the scheme became apparent. The details of the diplomatic negotiations during these years are not known. It is said that France at one time offered to build a route from Homs on her Beirut-Damascus line to Bagdad without a guarantee, but the protests and counter proposals were unavailing and the convention was drawn up and published.

The storm then broke loose with renewed fury in England and France. Debates ensued in the House of Commons and in the Chambre des Députés, and in both the decision was reached not to accept the offer of the German syndicate for participation in the scheme. The English government seemed at one time indeed favorably disposed towards sharing in the railway as a means of making her influence felt and safeguarding English interests, but the popular opposition roused to a high pitch of indignation at the failure of the government to prevent the convention from being consummated, forced Balfour at the time Prime Minister, to abandon further negotiations. Moreover, there seemed to be no prospect of securing for England a place in the enterprise on an equal footing with the German and French capitalists. This was in April, 1903. A little later, after a violent debate in the French Chambre, the decision was reached that the bonds of the Bagdad Company were not to be quoted on the Paris Bourse. In France the inclination of the government was likewise to participate, with the understanding that French capital was to be represented by 40 per cent., equal to that of the German syndicate, and the balance, 20 per cent., to be accorded to some power— presumably Russia. Charges were brought against M. Delcassé, then Minister of Foreign Affairs, that he and the French Ambassador at Constantinople, M. Constans, had abetted Germany in her negotiations with the Porte. This suspicion was probably a factor in leading to the final action which was, to be sure, in the nature of a compromise, for it permitted French capitalists to invest if they so felt inclined, without having the stock of the company listed on the bourse. As a matter of fact, French capital some years later—about 1910—became interested to the extent of 30 per cent. as against 40 per cent. of German capital, with the balance divided among Swiss and Austrian capitalists and banks. Since the latter groups worked in harmony with Germany, the German control of the entire enterprise remained undisputed.[17]

---

[17] According to the most recent data, the Directors of the company at the outbreak of the war consisted of 26, distributed as follows: 11 Germans, 8 French, 4 Turks, 1 Austrian and 2 Swiss, *i.e.,* 18 votes controlled by the Germans.

Looking at the action taken by England and France in the light of later developments, one is inclined to commend the wisdom of Balfour and Delcassé in favoring participation, and to regret that they could not carry through the negotiations in progress to a successful issue. Even with a preponderating German representation in the Directorate of the company, the presence of English and French capitalists would have acted as a check against designs to use the project for political aims, as their presence would also have enabled the English and French governments to watch the unfolding of plans in a direct manner, instead of being dependent upon reports and announcements after the *fait accompli*. There was also—it must be recognized—a justification for the German point of view that the control should not be transferred to a combination that might become strong enough to oust the German syndicate at some time in case of a crisis. The project, whatever its origin and its purpose, had taken definite shape in Germany. It was a creation of German enterprise and it had been made possible through German pressure at Constantinople and through the willingness of German capitalists to undertake it. Most favorable terms for investors had been secured through German influence at Constantinople, and under these circumstances the offer of the German syndicate to " internationalize " the enterprise should have been accepted on its face value and in good faith until evidence to the contrary had been forthcoming. The German syndicate was insistent through Dr. Siemens that there was no political aim attached to the project, and there was no reason to question *his* perfect sincerity in this view. The German government had given assur-

ances to the Sultan that it did not propose to use
the project for colonization purposes, though German
publicists foresaw that the increase of commerce
with the Orient would lead to large settlements of
Germans in Asia Minor, as commercial opportunities
had brought them in large numbers to Brazil and to
the Argentine Republic. Such a result, natural and
legitimate, could only be of benefit to the general
commercial and industrial progress of the world, as
long as it was not deflected towards carrying out
political aims. The German Chancellor von Bülow
had explicitly declared in 1903 that Germany was
not connecting political aims with the railway. Even
though this statement might have been made in
order to put the European powers off the scent, it
would still have been better for England and France
to have accepted the offer to participate, if for no
other reason than to be in a better position to watch
the game from the inside, instead of being forced to
peep through the fence.

VII

For France there was an additional reason for
participation because of her large holdings of railways
in Asia Minor and Syria which would all connect
eventually with the Bagdad Railway. Besides the
Smyrna-Kassaba line, transferred to a French company in 1893, and the Mersina-Adana line in which
French and English capital was interested (before referred to),[18] French capital and French enterprise had
built a railway from Jaffa to Jerusalem (86 kilometres, or about 54 miles) in 1892. A French Company
was organized in the same year for the building of the
Beirut-Damascus railway, later extended northward

---

[18] Page 87.

to Homs and Aleppo, and south to Mezerib, a total of 578 kilometres, or 361 miles, and completed in 1910.[19] Early in the century the French also constructed a railway from Tripoli to Homs, which was to offset in a measure the Bagdad Railway through the control of a second port on the Mediterranean by the side of Beirut. The French plans also contemplated the extension from Damascus to Jerusalem and thence through Bethlehem to Gaza.[20] At Aleppo the junction would be made with the Bagdad Railway and, via the section Aleppo-Damascus, with the starting-point also of the Hedjaz railway, built by the Turkish government for the benefit of the Mohammedan pilgrims. This road runs along a stretch of 1754 kilometres, or 1097 miles, to the two sacred cities of Arabia, to Medina where Mohammed died, and to Mecca where he was born.

---

[19] The section Damascus-Mezerib was opened in 1894; the section Beirut-Damascus in 1895, and the connection with Aleppo in 1906. There is also a railway Acre-Haifa to Damascus, opened in 1905, and under Turkish control, connecting with the Hedjaz Railway at Darat.

[20] Since the beginning of the war the connection of the Haifa-Damascus Railway has been extended by the Turkish government from El-Fule to Lydda, where a junction has been formed with the Jaffa-Jerusalem line. Beyond Jerusalem the railway has also been extended at least to Beersheba, perhaps to Bir Auja (according to Woods in the *Geographical Journal* for July, 1917, p. 54)—a total distance of about 160 miles. A part of this railway has been destroyed by the English army coming across the Sinai Peninsula from Egypt and which, according to recent reports, has taken Beersheba. Within the last two years the English have built a railway from Port Said along the coast to within about 10 miles from Gaza. Since the beginning of the war, the Turks have destroyed the Jaffa-Ramle section and the Tripoli-Homs railroad, to use the rails for the construction of the El-Fule-Lydda-Jerusalem-Beersheba stretch.

The Tripoli-Homs road had been built without any
guarantee or subsidy from the Turkish government.
It was the intention, moreover, of the French capitalists to carry on the Beirut-Damascus-Aleppo line
to Birejik and extend east to Adana, so as to connect with the southern coast of Asia Minor. This
plan was, of course, destroyed by the Bagdad Railway convention. Moreover, had the convention not
come in between, the French company would have
also extended the Syrian railway system to the southeast of Birejik, along the Euphrates, direct to Bagdad.
This plan had actually been worked out while
M. Paul Cambon was French Ambassador at Constantinople. The approval of the Turkish government had been secured, but the necessary capital
could not be obtained at the time and so the scheme,
which tallied closely with the English project of
Sir William Andrew,[21] was temporarily abandoned.

France had, therefore, good reasons for chagrin
and alarm upon the announcement of the convention
for the Bagdad Railway scheme, but an equally
strong reason for participating in it as a *fait accompli,*
because of the two junctions with French railways
at Afiun-Karahissar in Asia Minor, and at Aleppo
in Syria. Over two hundred millions francs of
French capital had been invested in these Asia Minor
and Syrian railways, besides one hundred and fifty
million francs represented by improvements in the
ports of Smyrna and Beirut, by the invested capital
of French commercial houses in Asia Minor and
Syria, and by the value of the holdings of French
religious and educational institutions in Palestine.[22]

---

[21] Above, p. 88.
[22] These are the figures for 1903, given by Chéradame,
Le Macédoine, Le Chemin de Fer de Bagdad, p. 262. No
doubt they have increased considerably since then.

Had France accepted the 40 per cent. of the total capital of the Bagdad Railway offered to her in 1902, or had France and England joined in accepting this share, equal to that to be retained by the German syndicate, the " internationalization " of the scheme might have developed amicably. That possibility at all events was the only hope of avoiding what did happen—the political exploitation of the scheme by Germany for enlarging her hold on Turkey and the East, and the endangering, in consequence, of the peace of Europe.

It would have been worth while to take the chance of participation instead of standing outside and allowing Germany free scope, which was no doubt what the German government wanted, though perhaps not the German capitalists who needed and sincerely desired outside co-operation. There is every reason to believe that at the end of the war, the " internationalization " of the Bagdad Railway will again be brought forward as the solution of the problem, and as the safeguard against using a great and valuable commercial enterprise for political ends. To be sure, it may be argued that the later investment of 30 per cent. of French capital with French representatives on the Directorate did not prevent political affairs from taking their course, but this capital came in at a late hour (about 1910). Moreover, it did not have the backing of the French government, and, therefore, lacked an important element of influence.

VIII

Meanwhile the railway began to be built and in October, 1904, the first section from Konia to Bulgurli was completed and opened a traffic. The construction of this section was, as pointed out, a comparatively simple matter and left a large margin of profit out of the guarantee for the concessionaires. The second and third sections, however, involved passage through a formidable mountain region with great engineering obstacles to be overcome that vastly increased the cost.[23] As against about 15½ million francs for the first section, the second was estimated to cost 75 millions and the third 40 million francs, while the cost of the fourth running again on a level surface would only be 22½ millions. Under the terms of the convention the loans were to be floated for one section only at a time. The company would, therefore, have only 54 million francs on hand (assuming a full return on the floated second loan) from which to build a section to cost 75 millions. A long delay now occurred with tedious negotiations and it was not until June, 1908, that a modification of the original convention was pushed through, whereby the plan of building only one section of 200 kilometres at a time was changed to a concession to build 840 kilometres, or 525 miles, from Bulgurli to El-Helif, not far from Mosul. The loan, covering almost three sections, was to be floated at one time, so as to place the full amount needed at the disposal of the company. Moreover, the company as a further concession was not obliged to begin building till 1911, at which time funds guaranteeing the interest on the enormous additional debt that Turkey was thus forced to take upon herself were available out of the *Dette Publique.* In 1911, finally, when work was resumed, a third convention was drawn up (March 20th), giving the concession

---

[23] See the account of these difficulties with illustrative sketch in Fraser, *Short Cut to India,* pp. 55-61.

for the 600 kilometres remaining from El Helif to Bagdad. Work was carried on at several points at the same time. At the time of the outbreak of the war in 1914, the second section from Bulgurli to Adana was almost finished, all but a small stretch of some 42 kilometres, or 26 miles, of particularly difficult construction to connect the two ends of the stretch.[24] The stretch from Bagdad to Samarra—120 kilometres, or 75 miles,—was also finished. Since the outbreak of the war, not only has the Bulgurli-Adana section been completed, but work beyond has been pushed to some 30 miles beyond Nisibin, within less than 100 miles, from Mosul, so that only this stretch and the one from Mosul to Samarra—a total of about 425 kilometres, or 265 miles,—is all that remains to complete the gigantic enterprise up to Bagdad.[25]

The long delay of almost seven years ensuing between the completion of the first section and the resumption of the work was not, however, due entirely to the financial difficulties. The opposition to the scheme continued and many things happened in Turkey to change the face of things. The Turkish revolution of 1908–1909 brought a different set of men to the helm. The growing complications in Morocco, which had not been simplified by the conference of Algeciras, constituted another factor suggesting to Germany to proceed cautiously. The

[24] From Dorak to Karapurnar work was carried on simultaneously at the Bulgurli and Adana ends. See *Geographical Journal*, vol. 44 (1914), pp. 577-580, with map. This stretch has now been completed.

[25] See Dominian, *Railroads of Turkey*, in the *Bulletin of the American Geographic Society*, December, 1915, and the references there given, the *Levant Trade Review* for June, 1916, p. 100, and the most recent account by Woods in the *Geographical Journal* for July, 1917.

agitation for an increase of the navy had also become more active during this period in Germany, occasioning further fears in England and Russia of Germany's future designs, while on the other hand the rapprochement between England and France, which received a strong impetus from the visit of King Edward to Paris, in May, 1903, was a forecast of the complete reconciliation between England and Russia, and had its natural reaction in making Germany feel that she was being encircled by Powers that wished to repress her ambitions.

The archives of the chancelleries of Europe, no doubt, conceal many negotiations and diplomatic conversations that took place during these years which have not as yet found their way to the public and perhaps never will. They would afford further explanations for the delay in the resumption of the project. Germany, more particularly, would be prompted to proceed slowly for fear of arousing a European conflict before she was ready for it. But while other issues in Europe and elsewhere were thus coming forward which contributed still further towards changing the political atmosphere until the storm of 1914 broke out, the most serious problem, though occasionally receding into the background, was ever that created by the suspicion of Germany's ambitions in connection with the Bagdad Railway. The growing influence of Germany in Turkey, strengthened if anything after the Turkish revolution, —for Turkey needed a powerful support for the two Balkan wars,—made England fear for the safety of the Suez Canal as well as for India. Russia realized that her hold on eastern Asia Minor and on lands beyond was threatened by Germany's plans.

Negotiations followed which at one time looked

BRIDGE OVER THE EUPHRATES AT JERABLUS ON THE BAGDAD RAILWAY

TERMINAL STATION OF THE BAGDAD RAILWAY AT HAIDAR-PASHA
OPPOSITE CONSTANTINOPLE

as though the European powers might avert the conflict which publicists and men of affairs felt was coming. To counteract the political influence of the Bagdad Railway, the general policy was advocated of building other railways in the disputed territory which through Russia's energetic policy in Persia had extended to that country. The French scheme of an Euphrates Railway from Damascus-Homs to Bagdad with connections to Tripoli, Beirut and Haifa, was taken up. This railway in French hands would offset Germany's ambition for a complete control of the highway of Asia Minor, since it would cut into this highway at a most important point. In case of war, French and English troops could be transported from three ports on the Mediterranean into Mesopotamia and secure that end. England was to be accorded the Bagdad-Basra stretch as her possession, while Russia was to be urged to carry out plans for railways in Persia which would include a line from Teheran to Bagdad. It is interesting to see in these plans their convergence towards one point—the Persian Gulf. Fully in accord with what we have seen to have been the primary factor in a control of the Near East, it was recognized that with the one pole of the wire stretching from Constantinople *via* Bagdad and the Gulf in the hands of England and her allies—France and Russia—Germany, holding Constantinople in her grasp through her alliance with Turkey, could never carry out her ambitions in the Near East, except by a military success over the Triple Entente of so decided a character as to force England, France and Russia out of the East entirely. This was in 1909–1910. In December, 1910, the English and French plans were laid before the Turkish government. The plan failed because of Russia's maintenance of her opposition to railways, and because Germany refused to give up the Bagdad-Basra sketch entirely to England, though Dr. von Gwinner in December, 1909, still contending that the entire undertaking was of an economic character, offered to English capitalists through Sir Ernest Cassel a controlling influence in that section. There was also an American project for obtaining railroad concessions in Asia Minor, brought forward in the year 1909, which was defeated by Russian and German influence in Constantinople.

For a time the situation looked more hopeful. England felt sufficient confidence in her ultimate ability to prevent any German control beyond Bagdad to encourage in the years 1909–1911, under the nominal auspices of the Turkish government, an elaborate investigation for scientific irrigation of Mesopotamia so as to redeem the country from the shameful neglect of Turkish rule, which for centuries had done little or nothing to maintain the canal system upon which the prosperity of southern Mesopotamia depended.[26] This investigation was carried on by Sir William Willcocks who formulated detailed plans for irrigation of large districts which, to be sure, could only be carried out at enormous cost but which would restore the country to its former splendor. A part of this work—the Hindia Barrage—was undertaken by Turkey and completed by the end of 1913. The

---

[26] As a result of this neglect great swamps are found in the southern Euphrates Valley, covering an area of over 50 miles in width and more than 200 miles in length. This swampy district, stretching to Basra, was one of the factors in bringing about the failure of the English campaign in 1915, since it prevented reinforcements sent to aid General Townsend from reaching him in time.

concession of March 20th, 1911, to build an additional section of the Bagdad Railway was limited to the stretch El-Helif to Bagdad. This seemed to accord with a definite agreement to which, according to Lord Haldane's recent account of strained relations between England and Germany during the years immediately preceding the war, the German Emperor had consented on the occasion of a visit to England in 1906, whereby England was to have the section from Bagdad absolutely. It is said, however, that the Emperor encountered opposition to the concession on his return to Berlin.

Another point secured in the year 1911 was the abandonment of Russia's opposition to the Bagdad Railway and her willingness to undertake railway construction in Persia to link on to the Bagdad line.[27] This change of the utmost importance took place as the result of a visit to the Czar to Potsdam in December, 1910, and was announced in August, 1911. Later, the reservations held by Russia for many years for the construction of railways in northern Asia Minor were turned over by her to a company of French financiers. A successful opposition on the part of England, France and Russia to an increase of custom duties in Turkey of 4 per cent., in order to provide more revenue needed to pay the interest of loans for the Bagdad Railway and which would have seriously impaired English and French interests more particularly, may also be listed as a gain. Negotiations to definitely settle other points of contention with Germany, more

[27] At Khanikin, to which a branch of the Bagdad line from Sadijeh was to be constructed by the Germany company. See above, p. 85.

8

particularly the ever crucial one of the stretch from Bagdad-Basra to the Persian Gulf, were in progress when the war broke out in August, 1914. It is reported that in July, 1914, an actual agreement had been reached, whereby England was to preserve her free scope at the Persian Gulf and her preponderance in that zone was to be unequivocally recognized. This must have involved, therefore, either the absolute British control of the stretch from Bagdad to Basra with no projection beyond to any port directly on the Persian Gulf, or a representation on the Directorate, of a character to safeguard English interests and to prevent the political exploitation of the enterprise—at least at the Persian Gulf.

IX

If this report be correct—and there seems to be no reason to question it—the outbreak of the war came at a particularly unfortunate time, for with the Bagdad Railway problem really out of the way, the entire Eastern situation would have assumed a far more hopeful aspect. The railway has been a nightmare resting heavily on all Europe for eighteen years—ever since the announcement in 1899 of the concession granted to the Anatolian Railway Company. No step ever taken by any European power anywhere has caused so much trouble, given rise to so many complications and has been such a constant menace to the peace of the world. No European statesman to whom the destinies of his country has been committed has rested easily in the presence of this spectre of the twentieth century. In the last analysis the Bagdad Railway will be found to be the largest single contributing factor in bringing on the war, because through it more than through any other cause, the mutual distrust among European Powers has been nurtured, until the entire atmosphere of international diplomacy became vitiated. The explanation for this remarkable phenomenon, transforming what appeared on the surface to be a magnificent commercial enterprise, with untold possibilities for usefulness, into a veritable curse, an excrescence on the body politic of Europe, is to be sought in the history of the highway through which the railway passes. The control of this highway is the key to the East—the Near and the Farther East as well. Such has been its rôle in the past— such is its significance to-day.

More is the pity that an undertaking which from every other except the political point of view spells progress, and which should have been the means of bringing the West back to the East, the daughter back to the mother and source of all civilization, should instead have led to the most violent struggle among the leading nations of the world in all history —a struggle in which all the gains made since the French revolution in the direction of the advancement of humanitarian aims, the betterment of the condition of the great masses, popular liberties and the progress in science and the arts, and all the efforts to bring nations closer to one another in a recognition of the common goal of mankind threaten to be dissipated. A railway which, as a medium of exchange of merchandise and of ideas, ordinarily fulfils the function of binding nations together, in this instance has been the primary cause of pulling them apart and of drawing them up in opposing camps, bent on mutual destruction.

X

To be entirely fair the blame for this outcome of the project must not be put entirely on the shoulders of Germany, though by far the major portion lies at her door. In the first place, there are no substantial reasons for assuming that when German capitalists began to develop their plans for a railway in a small section of Anatolia, they were actuated by another motive than that which had prompted English capitalists in earlier days to build a line from Smyrna, and French capitalists to undertake railways in Syria. Germany since the end of the seventies had moved forward by leaps and bounds in her foreign commerce as in the growth of industries within her borders. Commerce is progressive and looks ever forward to new regions to conquer. Before the present Emperor came to the throne, Bismarck had launched German colonization in southern Africa, as a natural outlet for surplus population and as a further medium of commercial expansion. German trade with the United States and with South America as with the Levant was growing. What more natural than that enterprising German capitalists should recognize the possibilities of an increase of trade through a railway across Asia Minor!

Railways are the natural means of opening up the resources of a country, and Asia Minor is particularly rich in natural resources and in fertile plateaus that under cultivation could become most productive. By the same natural process, England had come to the Persian Gulf and established her trade on a firm basis, and France had come to Syria. The thought of a further extension of the railway from Angora or Konia was equally natural, and it

will be recalled that the project of a railway to
Bagdad, connecting the Mediterranean with the
Persian Gulf first took shape in English brains and
came near to being realized long before Germany
had appeared on the scene.[28] Moreover, the original plan of the German syndicate, following the
scheme of Dr. Wilhelm von Pressel, the engineer of
the Anatolian Company, would have avoided any
conflict with English or French plans for a more
direct route from the Gulf of Alexandretta across to
the Euphrates. The northern route, if it had been
chosen, would never have led to an ambitious Pan-
Germanic program for a German control of the East,
which could only be carried out through the medium
of a transverse route for the Bagdad Railway, controlling the highway along the historical road from
Constantinople to the Persian Gulf. It was Russia
who was responsible for the change in the German
route which, as we have tried to show, made all the
difference in the political aspects of the enterprise.
The far more difficult and infinitely more costly route
from Konia across the Taurus range created the
international problem. One may question, therefore,
whether up to the close of the last century, German
capitalists were in league with a government having
ulterior motives of a political character in view in
pushing their project.

Exactly when the German government under the
leadership of the Emperor connected these motives

[28] The plan was again brought forward by Sir Wm.
Willcocks in 1910 (see *Geographical Journal,* vol. 35 [1910],
p. 13) in connection with his plans for the renascence of the
Euphrates Valley through an elaborate scheme of irrigation. The railway was to start at Tripoli and pass across
northern Syria via the Euphrates to Bagdad.

with the railway is a question difficult if not impossible to answer. In a general way the policy of expansion for Germany was an inheritance of the Bismarck period. It took on a larger aspect with the growing prosperity of the country, and no doubt was stimulated by the restless energy of the young Emperor—who was as progressive in everything that concerned Germany's advancement as he was aggressive in his whole attitude. The two traits are generally found united. But such aggression, taking on the formulation of plans for acquiring a foothold in the East, was entirely in line with the general policy of European nations, who from the beginning of the nineteenth century had gathered like hawks around a carcass, to divide up as much of the Turkish Empire as they could snatch. No doubt this appropriation has worked great benefits for the lands thus absorbed. Witness Algiers and Tunis and, more particularly, the marvellous transformation that England has worked for Egypt through her splendid and tactful régime, but the absorption, albeit beneficent, involved taking away the liberty of peoples to choose their masters. Germany was, therefore, in her policy, merely following the example set by others, and she had determined like Shylock to " better the instruction."

She did so, and seized upon the magnificent project of a railway that would form the shortest route through the Near East to the Far East and, connecting on its way with all the veins of the region marked by railways constructed or projected, would give her a dominant position among European powers. We may assume that some such idea was in the Emperor's mind when on his visit to

Damascus in 1898, he proclaimed himself to be the
" friend and protector of the three hundred millions [29]
of Mohammedans." He had a vision of the glorious
future in store for his country, extending its influence
over the entire East—even to distant India where
there are large numbers of Mohammedans, and naturally to Egypt. Utterances of such a mystic character,
coming from the Emperor, and given under a dramatic
setting,[30] did much to arouse suspicion of Germany's
ulterior designs in the Near East, and when such delphic
sayings were translated into language of unmistakable
clearness by boastful Pan-Germanic publicists, intoxi-
cated with enthusiasm over their far-reaching schemes,
the natural result was to arouse all Europe to the
menace involved in a control of the historic highway,
dominating the East by the strongest military power in
the world, and which was fast becoming also one of
the strongest naval powers. The terms of the convention when made public in the two forms in 1902 and
1903 clinched the situation, and left no doubt of the
decidedly political character that the enterprise had
acquired through the backing of the German
government.

Even then we need not assume that the German
syndicate was in league with the Pan-Germanic
movement. Capitalists—even though they be
patriotic Germans—are not apt to be carried away
by political visions. They realize the advantage of

---

[29] The figure was too large by about a hundred millions,
but that did not disturb his Majesty.

[30] The words were uttered under the shadow of the
tomb of the Sultan Saladin, the conqueror of Jerusalem, and
on whose grave the Emperor laid a wreath which was still there
in 1912, when I visited Damascus.

large enterprises for their country, but their point of view for all that is apt to remain financial rather than political. To the credit of leaders of finance in Germany, like Dr. von Gwinner, it should be said that they did all in their power to "internationalize" the undertaking, with the perfectly natural limitation of not wishing to see the project pass out of Germany's hands. Dr. von Gwinner was handicapped by the conviction that grew stronger year by year, that whatever the attitude of the German syndicate as business men might be, the German government was behind the plan with political ends in view. We have seen how the suspicion of this end grew apace, and despite occasional prospects of a settlement of the points of contention among the European powers, the inevitable conflict as a result of this suspicion set in.

XI

Such is the story of the Bagdad Railway which contributed more than any other complication to create the condition needed for the conflict. From the historical point of view there are thus two aspects to the Bagdad Railway. It represents, on the one hand, the last act in the process of reopening the direct way to the East which became closed to the West by the fall of Constantinople in 1453, and which began to be reopened with the loosening of Turkey's hold on one end of the historic highway stretching across Asia Minor. On the other hand, the conflict to which the railway gave rise illustrates once more the crucial rôle that this highway has always played in determining the fate of the Near East from the most ancient days down to our times. The opposition of the European powers to the Bagdad Railway, used as a political scheme for the aggrandizement of a particular country, registers the instinctive protest of the West against the domination of the East *by any one power*—no matter which. The danger would have been just as great and the hostility aroused just as strong if Russia had at any time seized Constantinople and threatened the East by an advance into Asia Minor, whether with an army or by means of a railway. The fatal error of Germany was to conceive of such a domination, for with the reopening of the Near East to the West, the logical plan, the one dictated by the verdict of history, was to keep the world's highway open for the *entire* West—and for the East. The Bagdad Railway in the hands of Germany, stretching from Constantinople *via* Bagdad to the Persian Gulf, would have meant the practical closing of the highway to all other nations—as effectively as the taking of Constantinople accomplished this in 1453.

The history of Asia Minor gives the verdict that the highway *must be kept open*—if the world is to progress peaceably and if the nations of the West are to live in amicable rivalry, while once more passing through the period of an exchange between Orient and Occident—such as first took place in the days of Alexander the Great. This verdict suggests " internationalization " of the highway as the solution, and it also voices a warning to the West that the reopening of the highway must not be used for domination over the East but for *co-operation* with it, not for exploiting the East, but for a union with it. What form that union should take will become clearer after a consideration of the two issues involved in the war.

CHAPTER IV
THE ISSUE AND THE OUTLOOK

I

THE war of 1917 is not the war of 1914; it is in fact an entirely different war. The terrific explosion of three years ago was the result of over-pressure exerted on the European body politic by conflicting national ambitions, by Pan-Germanism on the one side, by Pan-Slavism on the other, by growing mutual distrust and fears among European nations, leading to the Triple Entente to counterbalance the Triple Alliance,—the one combination as unnatural as the other was incongruous, and by economic rivalries. There were definite issues of a political, racial and economic character involved in the war that thus broke out, but these issues have all been moved into the background for the present by the paramount one that marks the war of 1917. The present war is *actually,* as has been so often set forth, a struggle on a gigantic scale for the preservation of popular government—and that is what that sadly overworked term " democracy " in its essence means —in those countries in which such government exists, and for the triumph of popular government in those countries in which it does not as yet exist. We are at war with Germany, because Germany represents a most powerful and a most menacing government, based not on the democratic but on the autocratic principle. The sinking of the Lusitania and the resumption of a ruthless sink-at-sight submarine policy represent the *occasion* for our entrance into the war, as the violation of Belgium's guaranteed neutrality on the part of Germany was the occasion for England's entrance. The *reason* in both cases lies deeper.

The change from the war of 1914 to that of 1917 was brought about by three factors: (1) by Germany's conduct of the war, (2) by the Russian revolution, and (3) by our entrance into the stupendous conflict.

Germany's diplomatic case at the outbreak of the war of 1914 was not bad. There was assuredly some justification for her feeling that she was hemmed in by hostile powers—by France and Russia. She had reason to fear Russian aggression, Russia being at the time in the control of a government of much the same autocratic character as that of Germany. With England and Russia pooling their interests in Persia in 1910, a new enemy had shown her hand, for it was the fear of Germany's growing power in the East that brought England to the side of Russia. The Agadir incident of 1911 revealed the definite alignment of England and France against Germany and foreshadowed the triple Entente, directed primarily against Germany. These facts must not be brushed aside in a review of the European situation, growing more complicated year by year, though it does not, of course, follow that we must accept Germany's interpretation of the facts. Germany saw France and Spain gaining control of Morocco, she saw Italy getting a slice of Turkey, and she was left out in the cold without the prospect of getting so much as a bone, if the plans of the European

powers arrayed against her were to be carried out.[1]
There was also some "academic" justification for
her contention that a quarrel between Austria and
Servia should be fought out by these two contestants, albeit that in reality the position taken may
have had a sinister substratum, but Germany entirely spoiled her case by her *conduct* of the war.

It is that conduct rather than her responsibility
for the war that has aroused at once the fear and
the hostility of practically the entire world, outside
of the groups arrayed on her side, and even these
groups stand in fear of her. In regard to the share
of responsibility for the actual outbreak of the war of
1914, there is still room for difference of opinion
even after three years of unprofitable discussion.
Certainly, the official mobilization of the Russian
army in the last week of July was a contributing
factor. No one who was in Germany at the time
when the mobilization of the Russian army was announced could have had any doubt of the genuine
fear of Russia felt in Germany. Germany could
have *prevented* the war, and that is quite as serious
a charge against her as the general belief that she
willed it.[2] In regard to her conduct of the war,

[1] When I was in the East in 1912, during the Turco-
Italian war, I heard much talk of a probable further partition
of Turkey's Mediterranean possessions, England to get or
take Palestine, and France to have Syria, and an agreement
that Germany was to have nothing. Of course, this may have
been *mere* talk, but I heard it.

[2] Her rejection of Sir Edward Grey's proposal for a
European conference to take up the Austro-Servian question,
when it was perfectly evident that the question without such
a conference would lead to a general European war, revealed
Germany's unwillingness to prevent war.

however, there can be no difference of opinion. The facts are there and speak for themselves. By Germany's conduct, I mean the military policy adopted by the General Staff and executed as the *official* acts of the German government, I mean the official violation of Belgium's neutrality, the official imposition of exorbitant fines on Belgian cities and towns, the official recourse to such mediæval, aye, almost primitive, methods of warfare as taking hostages and deporting the population of invaded districts,[3] the official order to burn and sack a large portion of Louvain, the official sinking of ships carrying noncombatants, the official destruction of towns and villages in the line of retreat, the *official* raiding of cities and towns by airships.[4] The feature common to these acts, apart from their inhuman aspect, is that

---

[3] This was the favorite policy of the ancient Assyrians.

[4] I exclude unofficial acts of individual soldiers, firstly, because such acts (violation of women, looting and individual deeds of cruelty) take place in every war. There are brutes in every army, and, secondly, because the accounts of such *individual* atrocities have probably been grossly exaggerated, as American newspaper correspondents traveling through Belgium at the time of the atrocities testify. Most of the cases in Lord Bryce's report on the atrocities in Belgium are *official* acts, not the doings of individual soldiers, acting from brute instincts let loose through the war. In the *Atlantic Monthly* for October, 1917, Professor Kellogg, of the American Belgian Relief Commission, while severely arraigning Germany's treatment of Belgium, expressly states that he came across no instances of Belgian children with their hands cut off or of women with breasts mutilated, despite the wide spread of such reports during the first year of the war and from time to time since then.

they affect to an almost exclusive degree the civilian non-combatant population. Their evident purpose was to terrorize and thus to reduce the *morale* of the enemy. They are *military* measures, and the German government so far from complaining of the hostility aroused by them ought consistently to welcome such hostility as an indication of the success of these measures. To be sure, the measures have also been stupid, for they have stimulated recruiting in England, have intensified the hatred of Germans in all the belligerent countries and have brought new opponents of Germany into the field—but they have, on the other hand, undoubtedly resulted in striking terror throughout the world and in bringing the entire world to the realization of the menace involved in the existence of a government acting autocratically, without any responsibility to the people and, therefore, without control.

II

Germany's military conduct is responsible for the present situation, and even those (if there be any) who would justify such conduct on the ground of military necessity, must recognize the *result* as a natural and logical sequence. The responsibility for *official* conduct rests with the German government and not with the people, who were not consulted either at the outbreak of the war or at any time during the war. The German government declared the war before calling in the Reichstag, and the same government is carrying it on, with little regard to the national legislative body which merely

passes the credits. Even the fact that the people
are patriotically behind the government does not
make the German people a *particeps criminis* in any
real sense of the word. That government has never
received a mandate from the people. It does not
act through the representatives of the people, but
imposes its authority on the population. In the case
of an autocratic non-responsible government, it is
proper to speak of the people *behind* the government;
in a democratic responsible government, the government is behind the people. In a democracy the
people lead and the government follows. In Germany, the government leads and the people *nolens
volens* must follow. The distinction between the
German government and the German people in the
official conduct of the war is, therefore, proper.

Such a distinction, entirely out of place in a popular government, is an inherent feature in a government imposed upon a people; and it makes little
difference whether we assume the German people
to be blinded, cowed, obstinate, politically immature,
or poisoned by mischievous and insidious theories of
the state, it is the government that must assume the
responsibility for the results of the policy adopted
by it. Besides, we must bear in mind that for many
years before the war, there was a continuous struggle in Germany for democratization, chiefly on the
part of the Socialists controlling several million
voters, and that at the outbreak of the war there must
have been over 50 per cent. of the German people
who were opposed to the form of government prevailing in Germany. The 107 Socialists in the
Reichstag, now joined by the Clericals (about 90)
and some of the liberal factions, constitute a major-

ity, fighting autocracy in Germany and determined to bring about that internal change which is a necessary preliminary to any peace negotiations.

Germany's conduct of the war, shameful and inexcusable, is thus the chief factor in creating the war of 1917—which may be defined as a realization of the fact that there is no room in the modern world for autocracy, especially if that autocracy be powerful and efficient. Nations cannot live on equable terms with one another in the present age of close intercommunication unless they are all organized on a basis of popular government. That kind of government is the spirit of the age, and the German government in opposing itself to that spirit becomes the enemy of mankind. The war of 1917 is, therefore, a struggle forced upon the world to secure the triumph of the spirit of democracy.

III

The significance of the Russian revolution lies similarly in revealing the strength of the spirit of the age in a country, which at the beginning of the war in 1914 was still striving to suppress it. Revolutions come ordinarily before a war or after a war. The almost unprecedented occurrence of a great revolution during a great war was a signal that the war for the triumph of democracy was about to replace the earlier one. It came at a time when Germany's conduct of the war had shown the menace involved in a government that was in opposition to the spirit of the age. The Russian revolution was not only a revolt against a government that had imposed a war on its people, precisely as Germany had imposed it, for the purpose of carrying out plans of aggression at the expense of other nations, it was the first decisive stroke for the triumph of world democracy. It revealed the existence of forces, lying deeper than the issues which brought on the war of 1914. It showed the *real* cause for the " European Anarchy," so forcibly described by Lowes Dickinson in his survey of the situation before 1914. That cause lay in the existence of governments which made their plans independently of the will of the people. The Russian Duma, though designed to have more authority than the German Reichstag, had become an offense to a government that was determined to make it its tool, and for a time succeeded in doing so. The spirit of autocracy was still strong enough in Russia in 1914 to ride roughshod over the principle of popular government, but the real issue, concealed for the time being by complications of a diplomatic character, rose to the surface during the war of 1914 and helped to bring on the revolution.

The present Russian government, entirely popular in character, has no concern with the issues of 1914. It therefore, naturally and consistently, renounces all plans of annexation and aggression which occupied the now overthrown autocratic government. It has no designs on Constantinople, nor is it concerned with the formation of a great Pan-Slavic state that would have been as serious a menace to the tranquillity of the world, as the carrying out of the ambitions of the German government for a " place in the sun," which would have thrown the rest of the world into the shadow. Russia is fighting for the preservation of its democracy, and its best leaders realize that this democracy is not safe as

9

long as an autocratic government is maintained in a neighboring state. Whether these leaders can guide the country through the present crisis remains to be seen.

Finally, our entrance into the war clinched the situation and gave to the war of 1917 its definite character as a struggle for the preservation and triumph of democracy throughout the world. The President of this great Republic has become the spokesman of the world. His peace and war messages alike breathe the spirit of democracy. A true statesman does not act upon "academic" theories, formed in his study, but from a profound recognition of the *meaning* of the events as they transpire. Led step by step through his interpretation of actual occurrences, President Wilson has reached his present commanding position, which has found its most notable expression in his answer to the Pope's proposals for peace. He has made the program of the war of 1917 so clear that he who runs may read. He has clarified the issue in such a manner as to make it evident even to the people of Germany that our war—the world's war—against Germany is *actually* a war for the German people, as much as a war for the preservation of American democracy. We as Americans have no special concern with the issues that brought on the war of 1914; we are solely concerned with securing the peace of the world through the establishment of popular government in Germany. The precise form of that government must be left to the people of Germany who will work it out in accordance with their special genius, but the *basic* principle of that government must be the same as prevails in democratic governments elsewhere—the complete responsibility of a

government to its people through its elected representatives.   Such is the war of 1917, clearly set
forth by the attitude of Russia and of the United
States; set forth with almost equal definiteness by
recent utterances of such leading English statesmen as
Lloyd George and Arthur Balfour, and which ere
long must be fully accepted as the issue by France
and Italy. How small and petty seem purely
national ambitions or measures of revenge after the
war in the light of the great paramount issue which,
in the President's interpretation of this war, stamps
it as one of the noblest as well as one of the most
dreadful of all wars—noblest by virtue of the issue
involved, dreadful in that the leading exponents of
modern civilization should still be obliged to have
recourse to the most barbaric manner of securing
the triumph of a great ideal.

IV

In contrast to the war of 1917, which may be
called the world war for democracy, the war of 1914
is the European struggle for supremacy.   Had this
latter war taken the ordinary course, it would have
shaped itself as a supreme struggle between England and Germany.[5] If England had triumphed,
there would probably have been a combination of
Germany and Russia against England. If Germany
had succeeded in imposing her authority on Europe,
the combination against her would have continued
and would have led in time to an attempt to throw
off the yoke—probably with the additional help of
the United States and China and the South American

---

[5] See the closing paragraph in Cramb, *England and Germany*, p. 136.

Republics. In either case the world would have been involved for years to come in preparations for another war, and militarism would have become rampant everywhere. The causes that led to the explosion in 1914 were of the ordinary kind—that is to say, the kind that ordinarily lead to wars. They have in the main been indicated above,[6] but there were two striking features marking the outbreak of the war. In the first place there were the premonitions through the aggressive spirit of both Germany and Russia, closely allied with the complications in the Balkan States, and in the second place the surprisingly large number of supplemental issues that converged to intensify the struggle for supremacy into a general melée on an unprecedented scale.

The Moroccan situation on two occasions within the last decade became threatening through Germany's ambitions, while the Balkan wars had a larger significance because of the face of Russia to be seen in the background. England's and Russia's interference in the affairs of Persia was another premonitory symptom, as was Italy's seizure of Tripoli. Again, the outbreak of the war at once revived other issues like that of Alsace-Lorraine for France, the Trentino provinces for Italy, Finnish independence, the dream of a resuscitation of Poland, the hopes of the Jewish Zionists for the possession of Palestine. Added to all these issues was the Bagdad Railway project which, as we have seen, developed from a commercial undertaking of the first magnitude to a political scheme of even greater proportions. This transformation in the character

[6] Page 123.

of the project was, as I have tried to show, gradually brought about through two factors (1) through the natural growth of Germany's political power as a consequence of her marvellous industrial expansion and which led her rulers to cherish political ambitions which were *unnatural,* because they transgressed bounds dictated both by existing circumstances and by due consideration for the peace of the world, and (2) through the close alliance between Germany and Turkey, which had led to the reorganization of the Turkish army under the tutelage of German officers.

This movement dates back to 1885, when the German General von der Goltz was called to Constantinople by the Sultan Abdul Hamid to become a professor in the chief military school of Turkey.[7] Others followed to assist von der Goltz, but it was not until after the Turkish revolution of 1908–1909 that a further stimulus was given to the movement by the appointment of a military commission of thirty German officers to train the Turkish army in German military discipline and German methods. The results are to be seen in the present war, in which the military strategy of the Turkish armies is carried out under the direction of German officers. The Turkish army is practically an adjunct to the German military machine.   An alliance between two nations, so diverse as the Germans and the Turks, naturally had an exclusively political significance

---

[7] It is worth nothing, however, that fifty years earlier (in 1836) Moltke, then a young officer in the Prussian army, spent over two years in Constantinople at the request of the Sultan Mahmud II, in imparting military instruction and in organizing the Turkish militia.

that still further demonstrated the intention of the
German government to use the Bagdad Railway for
carrying out its political ambitions. The historic
highway across Asia Minor, thus controlled by the
military staff of Germany, would be closed to the
rest of Europe. The railway would serve as a
barrier as effective as the one erected by the Ottoman
Turks, when by the taking of Constantinople they
controlled the entire stretch to Bagdad and the
Persian Gulf. If anything was needed to bring
the various issues agitating Europe to a convergence,
the situation created by the political character given
to the Bagdad Railway was able to do so. One of
the articles in the convention of 1902–1903, granting
the concession of the line to Bagdad, stipulated
that the road was to be used by the Turkish government for military transportation, and the German
company had to pledge itself to build military sta-
tions along the route, at an expenditure up to four
million francs. The stipulation was perfectly natural, but the reorganization of the Turkish army
under German tutelage changed the character of
the article in the convention to a German military
measure, which would give Germany not a commercial but a military support for the exploitation of the
East. It could lead to nothing else but to the control of the entire Nearer East. With Asia Minor
in her hands, Germany would be in a position to
follow in the wake of ancient Persia, Greece, Rome
and the Arabs, and to have Mesopotamia, Syria,
Palestine and Egypt fall into her lap.

Through the Bagdad Railway events were thus
shaping themselves for a terrific conflict in the East
that would parallel the coming clash in the West.

The addition of the Bagdad Railway project to the Eastern question rendered the outlook for any satisfactory settlement of that question practically hopeless. The gathering clouds became more ominous, and despite occasional rifts they grew thicker and steadily descended.

Since the Agadir incident in 1911, it was more clearly evident than ever to careful observers that the hopes for a peaceful solution of the many problems presented by European politics had diminished. Only wise counsels or the rise of a great commanding figure in some European capital could have averted the catastrophe which was " on the cards." Without either contingency it was only a question of time before Pan-Germanic ambitions, contemplating a sphere of influence stretching from Berlin across Vienna and Constantinople to the Persian Gulf, would clash with Pan-Slavic policies for the creation of a confederacy of Slavonic States under Russian domination, or before Germanic expansion would lead to a life-and-death encounter with England, with the slumbering yet potent hostility between Germany and France ready to be aroused by either outbreak. Wise counsels did not prevail either in St. Petersburg or Vienna, nor did the great statesman with a large vision appear either in London or Paris or Berlin, and so when the fatal last week of July, 1914, arrived, the scene was set for the tragic climax to the futile negotiations of the diplomats.

V

The issue of 1917 will have to be settled before those of 1914 can be taken up. So much is evident from the profound change that has come over Russia and from the entrance of the United States into the war. President Wilson's answer to the peace proposals of the Pope has committed this country definitely to the policy of first making " the world safe for democracy " before taking up the issues involved in the war of 1914. It is only a question of time— and perhaps a short time—before the Allies will clearly and unequivocally accept this policy, and make the sacrifice of placing their claims and hopes for the time being into the background in order to win the paramount issue—the overthrow of a mediæval form of autocratic government in Germany, and the substitution of a form that will recognize as its central principle the responsibility of a government to the constituted representatives of the people. The details are unimportant. The recognition of the principle is the essential thing. It is hardly necessary to argue that the preliminary condition, so forcibly set forth by President Wilson, does not involve any interference in the internal affairs of a nation. The democratization of Germany is precisely what the liberal element in that country, representing even before the war a majority of the people, was striving for; and this proportion has increased since the war, as is evident by the defection of the Centrum party, which before the war was always to be found on the side of the government. It is, therefore, entirely accurate to say that the issue of 1917 is being fought for the benefit of the German people as much as for the safety of the world. The danger for us lies in a confusion or a commingling of the issues of 1914 with the *single* one of 1917. With the issues of 1914 we as a nation are not concerned. They arose in Europe and belong to Europe, but for that very reason we will be in a stronger position to advocate at the peace conference a solution that will be just, and one that will give due consideration to avoiding the repetition of the conditions that brought on the war.

The adjustment will be difficult but not hopeless after once the atmosphere shall have been cleared of the vitiated currents created by the poisonous gases of an irresponsible autocracy, using as its weapon military terrorism. The world will breathe more freely after Germany shall have adopted or shall have by circumstances been forced to adopt the principle of popular government, and thus be placed on a par with conditions prevailing in all other civilized governments at the present time—though under varying forms. Political intrigue, and political plots, including an elaborate and sinister " spy " and " agent " system are the tools that an autocracy needs to maintain itself in opposition to the will of its people. Russia before the war used precisely the same tools—only not so cleverly and perhaps not so lavishly as Germany. A government that receives its mandate from the people, that derives its authority from the popular will and that makes its account to the people does not need such methods—it spurns them. An autocratic military government is necessarily bent upon perpetuating itself; a democratic popular form of government is necessarily bound by the will of the people. A free people does not favor conquest at the expense of enslaving another people; it will not tolerate a policy that creates the atmosphere of war. Democracy, to be sure, is liable to error and not infrequently falls into error, but the inherent sense of

right and justice in the people will assert itself
sooner or later—and generally sooner than later—to
correct the error. An autocracy regards itself as
infallible. It knows no law the fulfilment of which
might endanger its own existence or its hold upon
the people. In a democracy law is supreme; in an
autocracy the law is bent to serve the purpose of the
rulers.

With all the nations engaged in this gigantic struggle—to safeguard and promote popular government towards which the entire civilized world has been tend-
ing—including, of course, Germany—since the French
Revolution, it is impossible for nations to live on terms
of peace with those that have not yet accepted the
underlying principle of democracy. In its last
analysis, the fundamental cause of the *kind* of war
that is now being waged was the existence of an
undemocratic government in one of the sister nations
—and that one of the most powerful and efficient, and
in all other respects one of the most advanced. One
cannot go so far as to assert that the issues of the
war of 1914 which were real and fundamental would
not have led to an outbreak if Germany had been
organized on a democratic basis, but the war would
have been fought out in an entirely different way.
It would not have led to the war of 1917.

VI

With the paramount issue won, the world will
be in a position to take up the issues of 1914, some
of which are of comparatively recent origin, like the
Alsace-Lorraine question or the problem of Finnish
independence, others of long standing like the Polish
question and the situation in the Balkan States,

which may be traced back to the foundation of the Ottoman world empire in the fifteenth century.

It is perhaps safe to predict at present, even before the *paramount* issue has been disposed of, that although there will be some readjustments, the map of Europe will not be materially changed after the peace conference has done its work. Belgium will be on the map as before the war, Finnish independence will be restored by a Russian Republic that will have neither the interest nor the desire to dominate a foreign nation. The one radical change to be expected in northern Europe will be the creation of an independent kingdom of Poland with its neutrality guaranteed. There may be a series of "internationalized" independent states, Belgium, Luxemburg, Lorraine and Alsace to form a continuous barrier between Germany and France,[8] and

---

[8] This solution appears to find much favor in England and might prove to be more satisfactory for the peace of the world than the alternative of allowing Lorraine and Alsace to decide by a referendum to which government each desires to be connected. We must not forget that while Lorraine is French, Alsace is at least as much German as it is French. It was German before it became French. See Dominian, *Frontiers of Language and Nationality in Europe,* p. 42, who says "Alsace was a province of German speech throughout the Middle Ages as well as after Louis XIV's conquest of the land. The French took a solid foothold mainly after the Revolution and during the nineteenth century. An enlightened policy of tolerance towards Alsatian institutions cemented strong ties of friendship between the inhabitants and their French rulers."

The entire third chapter in this admirable book on *The Franco-German Linguistic Boundary in Alsace-Lorraine and Switzerland* is an important contribution to the subject, which should be carefully read by those interested.

whose neutrality will be guaranteed by all the nations of Europe combined, or by the League of nations which may be formed after the war. There may be some alteration of the boundary between Italy and Austria, along the lines of concessions which Austria was ready to make at the outbreak of the war during her negotiations with Italy. It may be that a confederacy of the Balkan States will be formed, and that Greece will obtain possession of all the islands in the archipelago, which by natural conditions belong to her.

In the Near East, however, momentous changes are to be expected. He would be bold, indeed, who would venture to predict of what nature they will be. All that I propose in these closing pages is the more modest attempt to forecast the *outlook* at the time of the Peace Conference. In the deliberations of the Peace Conference to which the world is looking forward so anxiously, the future of the countries lying around the Mediterranean Basin will constitute the most serious problem to be considered. It is a problem far more intricate than any of the issues in the West. The prerequisite condition to a satisfactory settlement is the determination of the principles that should guide the deliberations of the conference. What these principles should be is suggested by the history of Asia Minor which is, as has been so constantly emphasized in this study, the key to the Near East.

Let us in the first place recognize that the extension of Western civilization into the East is as inevitable as was the peopling of the Western Continent by settlers from Europe, consequent upon the voyages of discovery four centuries ago. The " trend

towards the East" which we have traced back to
the days of Alexander the Great, which actuated
Rome and which underlies the movement represented by the Crusades, again set in at the end of
the eighteenth century when Napoleon brought his
armies to the base of the pyramids of Egypt. That
expedition foreshadowed the removal of the barrier
set up by Mohammedanism against European and
Christian access to the East. The Western invasion
of the East has been going on steadily since that
time and will receive a fresh stimulus through the
present struggle.

But this important distinction between the earlier and the recent "trend" is to be noted. Until
the last effort of the Crusaders to keep the way to the
East open to the West, the West was attracted to the
East for what it could bring *out* of it. The East
until the fifteenth century was still the treasure-
house of art, of artistic manufacture, and of products essential to Western civilization. It had still
retained in a large measure its position as the mother
of all culture, for even Greek civilization was largely
Eastern in origin, having the stamp of the East on
it, and Rome was dependent for her art and her literature and her thought upon the stimulus she received
from the Greek models. The religion of Western
Europe was an eastern product, modified by contact
with Greek thought, that was unfolded under the
influence of Eastern ideas. The Arabs passed on
the torch of learning to the West. Even Greek
philosophy came to Christian Europe in the form
given to it by Mohammedan scholastics. Moorish
and Byzantine architecture—essentially Eastern—
formed the inspiration that led to the "Gothic"

as the notable expression of the Western spirit. The Mediæval mind was largely steeped in Eastern thought and in Eastern views of life.

In the modern " trend toward the East," on the other hand, it is the West that is pouring its products *into* the East. Commerce is based on exchange of wares, but what we are sending to the East far outbalances what we are extracting from there. Trade with the East in our days means bringing the West to the East. Europe and America measure their success in securing this trade by the increase of their exports. The tendency at least is all in the direction of filling the East with Western manufactures.

We are also introducing Western modes of transportation, Western inventions, Western methods of building, Western sanitation and Western ideas of education, as well as Western models of government. The East is being transformed under this influence of the West—slowly but surely; and travelers whose romantic natures are thrilled by the originality and picturesqueness of the disappearing East not infrequently lament the change,[9] which it must be admitted is not always to the advantage of the East. The tendency, however, is unmistakable, due to forces over which we have no control. It should be our task to *understand* this tendency, to recognize its deeper import, and to direct it by an intelligent policy into the proper channels.

---

[9] So Lord Redesdale in his charming " Memoirs " (London, 1916).

VII

What can the modern " trend " or rather, let us say, what should it be but the movement towards the *resuscitation* of the East?

The East made its last notable contribution in the seventh century of this era when it gave birth to a new religion, genuinely oriental in spirit and character. Mohammedanism swept through the world and led to a distinct civilization known as Arabic, which exercised a profound influence on European thought and science. This civilization ran its course to the climax during the six centuries following upon Mohammed. Since then the East has entered upon a state of languish, from which it has been occasionally roused as after the Crusades under the spell of the Ottoman conquests, but without making any further contributions to the world's treasure-house. The soil of the East had become exhausted after so many milleniums. Some new chemical element was needed to restore it to vigor. The conservatism which we are in the habit of associating with the East is merely a symptom of this languishing condition. The Ancient East was progressive, or it would not have produced the great civilizations that are being unearthed through the researches of the archæologist and the historian. The modern East is disillusioned, because it is so old. It has seen glory arise and fade away so often that it has lost faith in permanent progress, and has either resigned itself to a fatalistic attitude towards life, or sought refuge from struggle by a quiescent myticism.

But the West, yielding to the charm and allurements of the East, is being once more driven to the lands that are the source and the very inspiration of all our Western culture. The pressure comes in the form of commercial expansion, greed if you please, but it also assumes other garbs, as the missionary zeal to bring Western education, Western medical progress, hygiene and religious and political ideals to the East. Both movements, the commercial and the educational invasion of the East, have been going on side by side for a century. They both spring from a source deeper than any force that can be controlled by human efforts, but to our shame it should be said that instead of recognizing this source as the *real* incentive to the Western invasion of the old East, we have acted on the principle that the progressive culture of the West justifies a forcible conquest of the East. Availing ourselves of the growing weakness of the East, its inability to cope with the new forces developed by the West, we have considered it to be our destiny to bring the East under subjection to the West. European nations have grabbed and exploited the East. They have looked upon the East as a hunting ground and have vied with one another in bagging the spoils. And yet beneath all this, and despite the opposition, aye, the hostility that through the spirit of greed and rivalry among European nations has been aroused in the East, the process of the resuscitation of the East has gone on, at times silently, but also through the direct methods which have been followed with such signal success by the French in Algiers and Tunis, and by the English in India and Egypt. Full recognition should be given to the results of European domination, on the whole beneficent, in these lands. A large share of credit falls also to the educational institutions organized in Eastern lands by European effort—missionary efforts in the best sense under both Christian and Jewish tutelage —and that have been productive of such striking results, though as yet within restricted circles.

Is not the implication clear that in our policy towards the East, we should start from the interpretation of the force that drives the West towards the East? Beneath the impelling economic and in part sordid motives on the surface is the recognition that the East at present *needs* the West in order to be awakened to a new life. Political aims must be made subservient to this higher meaning of the modern " trend towards the East." Herein lies the fatal error of Germany in reversing the proposition, and making the trend subservient to political ambitions. Through this error she transformed what would have been an inestimable blessing into a dire curse. She is far from being the only sinner, but she has the misfortune of being the latest culprit. Her great chance of success in a political scheme of vast proportions that ran counter to the movement for opening up the East has been the means of rousing the world to the wrong course that we have *all* followed in our dealings with the East, and this despite great benefits that have been conferred on the Orient.

VIII

The West should seek the *co-operation* of the East. It should come as an awakener, not as a conqueror. The aim must be to bring to the East the best that the West has to offer, but not to attempt to make the East merely a profitable adjunct to the

10

West. Nor should we go so far as to dress up the East in Western clothes and produce a misfit. There is a decided sense in which

> "East is East and West is West
> And never the twain shall meet."

A resuscitated East must remain Eastern to bring about the best results. If the East has any further contributions to make—in art or science, in commerce or thought, or perhaps in the domain of religion in which she has given the world at least three-fourths of what religion there is, she can only do so through revivification—through the reunfolding of her own peculiar genius.

All this may sound "academic"—possibly utopian. Is there any practical policy to be followed upon the conclusion of the war to *rectify* the errors that have been made? I believe, yes. The story of the Bagdad Railway points the way out. Had the "internationalization" of the project been carried out at the start before an ambitious Emperor, arousing Pan-Germanic dreams, succeeded in attaching to the undertaking political aims which soon overshadowed the commercial and industrial aspects, there would have been no clash among European nations over the historic highway. That highway would have been opened up to the entire West, and the process begun by Napoleon completed to the benefit of the world—to the benefit of the East as well as of the West, and all nations would have had their share. "Internationalization" means *co-operation* among European and American nations, and such co-operation spells also partnership with the East, instead of domination . "Internationalization" in enterprises that are of importance to the world as a whole is a guarantee of mutual good faith, for where all share in the results, there is also a sharing of the feeling of responsibility. Internationalization brings home the conviction that the interest of one nation is bound up with the interest of all the others involved.

Ever since the decline of the Turkish Empire, Turkey has needed the support of European nations, and this support should have been given, not for the sake of Turkey, but for the sake of the East, of which Turkey was merely the chief symbol. Instead, Turkey has been exploited now by one group now by another. The European nations have been standing around the bedside of the " sick man of Europe " (as Turkey has been called) for half a century, quarreling over the division of the prospective corpse. It is not an edifying spectacle. But even if Turkey should die, the East would still be there, the various peoples of the East, the Turks, the Armenians, the Arabs, the Egyptians would still remain.

The weakness of the Turkish Empire should be interpreted as the call of the East to the West to come to its support—to bring new life to it. The great opportunity will come at the close of the war. It rests with the West to direct the momentous changes which the East is forced to face into a channel that will lead to its resuscitation. The policy of " internationalization," so plainly suggested by existing conditions in the East, should at least be given a trial. Let a beginning be made with the reorganization of the Bagdad Railway on a basis which will divide the investment among the capitalists of various nations interested, with *equal* repre-

sentation in the Board of Control. That will be the
first important step towards opening up the great
highway to all. Asia Minor is the world's highway.
It should be secured for the benefit of the world.
The fate of the East, dependent upon the control
of the route stretching from Constantinople to the
Persian Gulf, should not be at the mercy of any one
nation.

The proposed policy would further involve the
"internationalization" of Constantinople under the
protectorate of an international commission, with a
circuit around it, the neutrality of which should be
guaranteed not by a few Powers but by the concert
of nations. Internationalization has been tried in
the instance of the Danube commission and has
worked satisfactorily. Why should it not apply to
Constantinople as the starting-point of the great
highway? Sir Edwin Pears, whose life-long residence in Constantinople makes him a valuable witness to the needs of the East, has been advocating
its "internationalization" since the beginning of the
war, and the plan is meeting, one is given to understand, with favor in France. The overthrow of
autocracy in Russia strengthens the claims for such
"internationalization" of the historic city on the
Bosphorus. Constantinople in the hands of Russia
would never have led to a solution of the Eastern
Question. On the contrary, it would have complicated it by another aggravating factor. The Russian Revolution has repudiated the policy of
conquest, which was a part of the old régime.
Russia, the republic, has no interest in holding
Constantinople, if under an "international" protec-

torate the passage through the straits will be open to all nations. Mesopotamia, Palestine and Arabia should likewise be placed under an " international " protectorate, and its populations be given the opportunity of developing their capability for autonomy, which at present they do not possess. Let England after the war resume the *protectorate* over Egypt which she has held for so many years, and encourage the education of the population so as to fit them for Home Rule; and France should do the same for Algiers and Tunis. The " internationalization " of Morocco, begun some years ago in a tentative fashion, should be made more definite, as a guarantee against a partitioning which would be an injustice. Finally, Turkey should again become what she originally was—an Asiatic empire. Her fatal error, as we have seen, was the attempt to become also a European power. That ambition led to her decline. The natural capital of Turkey is Konia (the ancient Iconium), which the Seljuk Sultans had chosen as their residence. The policy of " internationalization " should be extended to Armenia, which should be organized as a separate state under the protection of the concert of nations, and Persia should be freed from all semblance of foreign domination [10] and her neutrality similarly guaranteed by *all* the powers.

---

[10] The flagrant wrong done to Persia in 1911 by Russia and England must not be glossed over. It needs to be undone thoroughly and unflinchingly. Brandes comes close to the truth when he calls Persia " the Asiatic Belgium." (*The World at War*, p. 250.)

IX

Under such conditions, the resuscitation of the East will proceed slowly but surely. The Western spirit of enterprise will open up the vast resources of the East. Irrigation systems in the interior of Asia Minor and Mesopotamia will restore and increase the fertility of these regions. Mines and wells will yield their treasures. Trade with the East will continue to grow in amicable rivalry. Western methods of self-government will make their way and a fresh impetus given to the education of the masses in the East. New problems will assuredly arise, and international crises will occur in the future as they have in the past, but with the spirit of co-operation between West and East, replacing the ambition to conquer and dominate, there will be a reasonable hope that these critical periods will be passed without plunging the world into internecine warfare.

It may be looking forward to Utopia to visualize the time when swords will be beaten into ploughshares, though there is no inherent reason why settlements of differences among nations by the ordeal of battle should not give way to other methods. Indeed, it may be confidently asserted, that unless as an outcome of the present war for democracy, a concerted effort for the ultimate abolition of war be made by the great nations who have it in their power to bring this about, the war will have failed of its purpose. For the world can never be "made safe for democracy" as long as the menace of war hangs over it. The spirit of democracy thrives in the atmosphere of pacifism. The deadliest foe to democracy is the militaristic spirit, which is always in danger of being engendered by war or, if it already exists, is in danger of being strengthened by war. The war of 1914 marks the explosion of the militarist spirit; the war of 1917 is the pacifist war, for democracy *is* essentially pacifism. The only kind of war that may justifiably be waged in the name of democracy is a war to *safeguard* democracy; and this means a conflict for the purpose of bringing us nearer to the end of all wars.

I am not concerned, however, with the distant future, but only with the outlook suggested by the present sad and depressing, though far from hopeless, conditions. *Dies diem docet.* The world proceeds step by step, each step suggested or, if you choose, imposed by the experiences of the past. The story of the Bagdad Railway as the crux of the Eastern Question during the past twenty years suggests as the next step— to give the policy of co-operation between East and West a trial. The results can assuredly not be worse than the mess created by the policy heretofore followed of exploitation, of conquest and of domination, leading to diplomatic intrigue, mutual distrust, political anarchy and—culminating in the war of 1914.

During the past century there have been three notable international peace conferences among European nations, which attempted to adjust the political problems of Europe and the East, the Congress of Vienna in 1815, of Paris in 1856, and of Berlin in 1878. A distinguished English writer [11] has recently pointed out the fundamental weakness of these Con-

---

[11] Sir John MacDonnell, "The Three European Settlements," *Contemporary Review,* September, 1917. The same view, practically, is expressed by Messrs. Hazen, Thayer and Lord in their *Three Peace Congresses of the Nineteenth Century* (Cambridge, Mass., 1917).

gresses in their neglect of the claims of the *peoples* whose fates were involved in the proposed settlements of disputed questions. Statesmen at these conferences rocked themselves in the delusion that by a shuffling and redistribution of the cards the world would move on smoothly. Only in the last of the three Congresses was a weak attempt made to consider the rights of a nation to lead its own life. The figure of Waddington, the French statesman, at the Berlin Congress, stands out conspicuously as the spokesman for the rights of the people, but the little that was accomplished was, soon after the Congress, nullified.

After the world has been made safe for democracy, it will be the chief task of the coming fourth Conference to *keep* it safe, by giving the first consideration to the claims of every people to life, liberty and the pursuit of happiness. The " old " diplomacy of 1815, 1856, and 1878 went bankrupt in 1914. The war to safeguard democracy should lead logically to a " new " diplomacy, based on the principles recently laid down by Sir Edward Grey, " The supremacy of right over force . . . and the free development under conditions of equality and conformity to their own genius, of all the states, large and small, who constitute civilized humanity." [12] If that spirit prevails —and the participation of the United States ought to be an additional guarantee that it will—the Eastern Question will finally be solved, because it will be *rightly* solved.

---

[12] See the extract from this speech (October 23, 1916) in H. A. Gibbons' *Reconstruction of Poland and the Near East* (New York, 1917), p. 66.

study of some of these fragments, Delitzsch laid the foundation for the scientific study of the Hittite language in a paper on Sumerisch-Akkadisch-Hettitische Vokabularfragmente (Abhandl. d. Kgl. Preuss Akad. d. Wiss. Philol. Hist. Klasse, Berlin, 1914, No. 3). This was followed by an investigation of an Austrian scholar, Friedrich Hrozny (Mitteilungen d. Deutsch. Orient Gesellschaft No. 56, May, 1916) which definitely established the Aryan character of the Hittite language. On the basis of the researches of Delitzsch and Hrozny further progress in Hittite studies will be rapid, when once the texts found at Boghaz-Keui shall have been published. It will then be possible to approach the decipherment of the hieroglyphic inscriptions with a surer hand. A preliminary study of the Hieroglyphic Hittite inscriptions which marks a distinct advance over former attempts was made a few years ago by R. C. Thompson, *A New Decipherment of the Hittite Hieroglyphics* (London, 1913).

(P. 38). The presence of Aryan settlements at an early period in Asia Minor is indicated also by the occurrence, in the clay tablets found at Boghaz-Keui, of the names of Hindu gods like Indra, Varuna and Mithra and the dioscuri Nasatjas, and of Aryan words like mariana "young man." This was first pointed out by Winckler, *Vorläufige Nachrichten über die Ausgrabungen in Boghaz-Keui im Sommer,* 1907 (Mitteilungen d. Deutschen Orient Gesellschaft, No. 35, December, 1907).

(P. 40). Supplemental to Egyptian, Babylonian and Assyrian records, we have a remarkable archive of official correspondence of governors of Palestinian towns and districts during the fifteenth century, with Egyptian Pharaohs under whose suzerainty they stood. These archives, found at Tel el-Amarna in Egypt and consisting of several hundred tablets—of official letters—shed much light on conditions in Palestine and Assyria during the fifteenth century before this era, with the Hittites as the chief disturbing element. Furthermore, we have the archives found at Boghaz-Keui, consisting of many hundreds of clay tablets in the Hittite language, transliterated in the Cuneiform script, by the side of many Cuneiform documents in the Babylonian language.

(P. 40). These tablets are generally spoken of as Cappadocian Tablets. Twenty-four of them were published a number of years ago by Golenischeff *Vingt-Quatre Tablettes*

Cappadociennes (St. Petersburg, 1891) and studied by Delitzsch, *Zur Entzifferung der Kappadokischen Tafeln* (Leipzig, 1894). Others have been published and studied by Sayce and Pinches.

(P. 46). On the remarkable religious reforms attempted by Ikhnaton, who proposed to concentrate the cult of Egypt on the sun-god Aton, see Breasted, *Ancient Times*, page 91 *seq.* and the interesting popular narrative of Ikhnaton's reign by Weigall, *Life and Times of Akhnaton, Pharaoh of Egypt* (Edinburgh, 1910). The king changed his name Amenhotep, containing the element Amon and which meant "Amon rests," to Ikhnaton, signifying "Aton is satisfied." Accompanying the religious reformation there was also a remarkable advance to a more realistic and less conventionalized art, hardly less significant as a sign of the age than the religious revolution which came to grief after Ikhnaton's death.

(P. 47). For the treaty between Hattusil and Rameses II see Messerschmidt's monograph, *The Hittites* (English translation, published by the Smithsonian Institution, Annual Reports, 1903, pp. 681–703).

(P. 47). See Breasted's monograph, *The Battle of Kadesh* (Chicago, 1903) for the strategic details of the battle, with full details of the pictorial and written material, including a poem composed by an ancient Egyptian on this famous battle.

(P. 49). For the details of Babylonian and Assyrian history the reader is referred to the two volumes of L. W. King's *History of Sumer and Akkad* and to R. W. Rogers' comprehensive work, *History of Babylonia and Assyria* (6th edition) (New York, 1916, 2 volumes); for an excellent survey of *The Ancient History of the Near East* (Egypt, Babylonia, Hittites, Assyria, Syria and Palestine) to H. R. Hall's work under this title (New York, 1913).

(P. 50). Owing to the sluggishness of the flow of the Euphrates which receives few tributaries after it leaves its mountain source, and to the deposits which are brought along by the down-wash, the river, choked up at one point, is often forced to seek a new bed as an outlet.

(P. 50). Ashur was the capital of Assyria till c. 1300 B.C. when it is replaced for a time by Calah, a little to the north. Nineveh, still further north, did not become the capital till 1100 B.C., and not permanently so till the reign of Shalmaneser III (858–824 B.C.). See Jastrow, *Civilization of Babylonia and Assyria*, p. 25.

(P. 51). I follow Breasted's figures for Egyptian history, as given in his standard work, *The History of Egypt* (New York, 1909) and *Ancient Times, A History of the Early World* (Boston, 1916) which, written in a most fascinating manner and elaborately illustrated, cannot be too highly recommended to anyone who wishes to obtain a view of the earliest civilizations of maniknd.

(P. 52). The "sons of Heth" from whom Abraham purchases the cave of Macpelah (Genesis, Chapter 23) are our Hittites, and while the story is of late origin, and the tradition is introduced with a view of legitimatizing the claims of the Hebrews to a sacred spot, such as the cave must have been, the substratum of the tale, assuming an early possession of the region around Hebron by Hittites, may nevertheless be sound and is confirmed by other evidence of the early penetration of the Hittites into Palestine.

(P. 55). See for a general account of Alexander's conquests, B. I. Wheeler's admirable work, *Alexander the Great* (New York, 1900) and Janke, *Auf Alexander des Grossen Pfaden. Eine Reise durch Kleinasien* (Berlin, 1904) for a detailed investigation of Alexander's routes in Asia Minor.

(P. 57). Excavations at Pergamon on a large scale were carried on by German archæologists, the results of which are set forth in a magnificent publication, *Altertuemer von Pergamon,* published by the German government (Berlin, 1885–1913).

(P. 58). Attalus bequeathed his possessions to Rome, which is to be taken as a "diplomatic" recognition of the *status quo,* just as Rome claimed that Alexander II (Ptolemy IX) had bequeathed Cyprus to her, as the justification for annexing it in 58 B.C. and as Ptolemy Apion in recognition of the inevitable had bequeathed the province of Cyrenaica on his death in 96 B.C. to Rome.

(P. 59). The rivers of Mesopotamia, and, more particularly, the Euphrates, bring with them a rich deposit from the mountain region through which they flow and which gives to the soil a remarkable fertility. The silt thus left behind adds steadily to the land. This growth of land at the

Persian Gulf goes on steadily at an astonishing rate. Cities which in the days of antiquity lay at the head of the Persian Gulf are now some 90 miles from the coast. When Bagdad was founded in the ninth century, Basra (or Bassorah), 500 miles south, was its port. Since then the accretion of soil has necessitated the creation of a second port, Fao—about 60 miles from Basra.

(P. 59). In connection with the annual deluge produced by the overflow of the rivers, it may be noted that the Biblical story of the Deluge, carried by the Hebrews to their later Palestinian homes, is based on the natural occurrence in Mesopotamia every year during the winter season, prior to the perfection of the canal system. The story is a nature myth, illustrating the change from the dry to the wet season, as the creation story marks the change from the wet to the dry season. See Jastrow, *Hebrew and Babylonian Traditions,* Chapter II. At present through the neglect of this system, large portions of southern Mesopotamia are annually submerged.

(P. 64). The best general work on the Turks is by Vambèry, *Das Türkenvolk* (Leipzig, 1885). Recent investigations of value are Cahun, *Turcs et Mongols* (Paris, 1896), E. H. Parker, *A Thousand Years of the Tartars* (London, 1895) and La Jonquière, *Histoire de l'Empire Ottoman* (Paris, 1914, 2 volumes). H. A. Gibbons, *The Foundation of the Ottoman Empire* (New York, 1916) is excellent for the period that it covers.

(P. 83). The full text of the convention, together with supplementary documents (in French), will be found attached to David Fraser, *The Short Cut to India* (London, 1909), pp. 316–381. The literature on the Bagdad Railway is most voluminous. Besides Fraser's book which goes fully into the subject, one may refer to André Chéradame, *La Macedoine, Le Chemin de Fer de Bagdad* (Paris, 1903) for the French view; to Paul Rohrbach, *Die Bagdadbahn* (Berlin, 1902) and Jaeckh, *Deutschland im Orient nach dem Balkankrieg* (Munich, 1913) for the German view. A good survey up to 1914 will be found in two articles of A. Géraud, *The Story of the Baghdad Railway,* in *Nineteenth Century* for May and June, 1914, and for the most recent developments in Dominian, *The Railroads of Turkey* (Bulletin of the American Geographical Society, 1915, xlvii, pp. 934–940), and H. Charles Woods, *The Bagdad Railway and Its Tributaries* (*Geograph-*

ical Journal, Volume L, July, 1917, pp. 32–57). For a general account of railways in Turkey see Coureau, *La Locomotive en Turquie d'Asie* (Brussels, 1895), George Young, *Corps de Droit, Ottoman* (Paris, 1906), or Chéradame's work. To make the record of railways in Asia Minor complete, it should be added that there is a small railway, built by a French company, of 41 kilometres, or 26 miles, running from Brusa, the ancient capitol of the Turkish Empire, to its port Mudania, on the Sea of Marmora, as indicated on the map. Though begun as far back as 1873, work on it was suspended and it was not opened until 1892.

(P. 98). The first of the brothers, Lieutenant Lynch, came with Colonel Chesney in 1835 to take part in a survey expedition of Mesopotamia. This expedition transported two small steamers, which they called The Tigris and The Euphrates, in pieces across the desert from a place near Antioch on the Orontes to the Euphrates at Birejik. The *Tigris* was lost in the difficult journey along the Euphrates, but the other boat reached the Persian Gulf and was the first steamboat to go up the Tigris. See Chesney, *Narrative of the Euphrates Expedition* (London, 1868).

(P. 105). The funds for the building of this road were obtained through contributions from Mohammedans in all parts of the world—an amazing example of the strong hold that the pilgrimage to Mecca still has upon Moslems and will no doubt continue to have. This obligation on every Moslem to pay a visit once in his life to the Holy City and perform the traditional rites creates a bond of union among Moslems, the strength of which cannot be overestimated. The railway to Medina (now completed) and to Mecca will by stimulating travel to the sacred cities tend to strengthen the hold of Islam on its votaries. The distance from Damascus to Medina is 820 miles. The entire stretch from Aleppo to Mecca is 1354 miles; from Damascus to Mecca, 1097. See on the Hedjaz Railway, Maunsell in the *Geographical Journal* for December, 1908, and in the *National Geographic Magazine,* Vol. 20 (1909), pp. 156–193 (richly illustrated).

(P. 112). See Sir Wm. Willcocks' *Irrigation of Mesopotamia* (London, 1911; 2 volumes—texts and charts). The scheme proposed is one of vast proportions, covering an area of one and a half million hectares to be affected by barrage works. Willcocks divided the proposed construction into six

divisions at a total estimated cost of twenty-nine million
Turkish liras. One of these divisions, the Hindia branch of
the Euphrates, was completed in December, 1913, and is now
in successful operation.

In this connection it may be interesting to note also
plans for developing irrigation in central Asia Minor. A German company has cut a canal from Lake Beyshehr to Chumla,
near Konia, to irrigate a tract of 12,000 square kilometres
and which will transform an arid wilderness into fertile
fields (*Levant Trade Review* for March, 1915, p. 353). This
work has been completed, and the Turkish government is
now considering plans for irrigation in the Cilician plain
which will greatly increase the cotton and sugar-cane crops.
The plans include the regulation of the water supply of three
rivers, the Saihun, the Jihan and the Berdanjaj. The total
cost is estimated at four million Turkish liras ($17,700,000).
See *Levant Trade Review* for June, 1916, p. 46.

(P. 150). The vast resources of Asia Minor, Northern
Syria and Mesopotamia can hardly be exaggerated. With
railroad connection and irrigation works (see note to p. 112),
the development of the natural wealth and fertility will be
the crucial factor in restoring the Near East to the position it
once held in the world. The northeastern region from Diarbekr to the shores of the Black Sea is rich in copper mines
(*Levant Trade Review,* June 16, p. 79), which will be opened
up through the projected railway to cover the stretch from
Angora-Sivas-Diarbekr with connections to Sinope and Trebizond on the Black Sea. The cotton crop in the province of
Adana for 1914 amounted to 120,000 bales. It is said that the
cotton industries of Adana supplied a large proportion of the
undergarments and summer uniforms for the Turkish army
during the present war. Through the proposed irrigation
scheme for the Cilician plain (see preceding note), the cultivation will be still further increased. The rug and the
fig industries in the district of Smyrna are among the
largest in the world. In Mesopotamia there are rich oil fields
and extensive asphalt deposits. Through irrigation works
in Mesopotamia the cereal products will again realize their
astonishing returns for which the region was famous in
antiquity. The irrigation of central Asia Minor will likewise
turn that region into a vast agricultural centre of untold
possibilities. See further Chapter VI in Fraser, *Short Cut to
India.*

DATE DUE

MAY 1 4